D1920416

Usborne Growing up for Girls

Felicity Brooks

Illustrated by Katie Lovell

Expert advice from:

Dr E Hothersall BSc MD FFPH

University of Dundee

Suze Lopez-Bradley Dip' Couns', MBACP

School Counsellor and Psychotherapist

Edited by Jane Chisholm

This edition first published in 2015 by Usborne Publishing Ltd, Usborne House, 83-85 Saffron Hill, London, EC1N 8RT. Copyright © 2015, 2013 Usborne Publishing Ltd. The name Usborne and the devices are Trade Marks of Usborne Publishing Ltd. All rights reserved. No part of this publication may be reproduced, stored in a retrieval system or transmitted in any form or by any means, electronic, mechanical, photocopying, recording, or otherwise, without the prior permission of the publisher. UKE. Printed in China.

Introduction

This book is about coping with puberty, which is the stage of your life when you start to change from being a child into an adult. Some parts of puberty may sound a bit scary, but they're much easier to deal with if you know what to expect.

Growing up isn't just about body changes. There are lots of changes going on in your brain too, so you have to learn how to manage new emotions and feelings. It's also the time when you begin to take responsibility for things such as your health, your schoolwork, what you eat, what you wear, planning your time, your safety, and relationships with your friends and family.

There's an enormous amount to learn, but these years can be fun and exciting as well as tough at times. Whether you've noticed some changes already, or are waiting for them to start, keep this book to hand to help you.

Contents

1. The puberty journey

People often talk about 'hitting puberty' as if it all happens suddenly one day when you're not expecting it. But really you start to change quite gradually and the changes carry on through your teenage years. It's a lot more like being on a journey than suddenly hitting a wall, and there are lots of stages, stops and starts along the way.

For girls, the most usual age to start is between nine and 13, but your body will begin developing at the time that is right and normal for you. Once you have started, there is nothing you can do to speed it up or slow it down (even if sometimes you feel you want to) so at times it may feel a bit like being on a roller coaster ride.

What happens?

As you grow up, there are all kinds of things going on inside and outside your body. Here is a list showing the order that these things most often happen, though everyone is different and these stages often overlap each other. Don't worry if you don't understand what some of this means as there's lots more about each stage in the rest of the book.

- You start to get bigger and taller.
- Your breasts start to grow.
- You become moodier.
- You get hairier and grow hair in new places.
- You start to sweat more.
- Your hair and your skin may become oilier.
- Your sex organs develop.
- You start your periods.

It can take over three years from the time you start changing until the time your periods begin. And after that it will be several more years until your body finishes growing up. (Your brain doesn't reach adulthood until about 25.)

1... 2... 3...

As you change from being a young child to a teenager, you may find you start to think and feel differently about things too. Try the quiz on the next page to find out where you are on your own puberty journey.

Quick quiz

- Do some activities, outings and games you enjoyed when you were younger now seem a bit babyish or boring?
- Do you find yourself suddenly losing it over little things and getting into silly arguments with your family and friends?
- Do you sometimes feel angry, stressed or a bit miserable for no obvious reason?
- Do your parents or carers drive you crazy (even when they are doing their best to be helpful and understanding...)?
- Do you feel self-conscious about your body?

Answers

Mostly 'YES' answers?
You are right in the middle of your journey and everything you feel now is completely normal. Try reading the 'Think tips' in this book to help you cope with your feelings.

Mostly 'NO' answers?
You may not have started your journey yet, but it won't be long. Keep reading to find out more about all the big changes on the way.

Some 'YES' and some 'NO' answers?
You have just started your journey and there are many exciting things ahead.

Think tip

When you are going through puberty, it can often feel as if nobody really understands. But it can help to remember that every adult you know has been through it, including your teachers, parents, aunts and even grandparents.

All your friends are or will be going through it too. Even celebrities have been through it (and some have made a fortune singing or writing about the experience). There are lots of ideas for how to cope with difficult feelings throughout this book.

2. Why is this happening to me?

If you're interested in why all this starts happening, here's the science bit.

All the changes that happen during puberty are caused by hormones. These are chemicals produced in glands inside your body and carried around in your blood. They act as signals that tell different parts of your body what to do and different hormones give signals to different parts.

Hormones aren't just concerned with puberty. Our bodies can make over 20 hormones and each has a different job to do. The hormone adrenaline, for example, is released when you are scared and it makes your heart beat faster and speeds up your breathing so you can run away if you need to.

You may have heard of a hormone called insulin. This works with another hormone called glucagon to control the amount of sugar in your blood.

The puberty trigger

The hormone which triggers puberty comes from a part of your brain called the hypothalamus. The hypothalamus is only the size of a grape and it is right in the middle of your brain, but it sets your body off on its puberty journey when you are asleep.

Once your body is ready, your hypothalamus starts releasing a hormone called gonadotrophin releasing hormone, or GnRH. This process always begins at night-time.

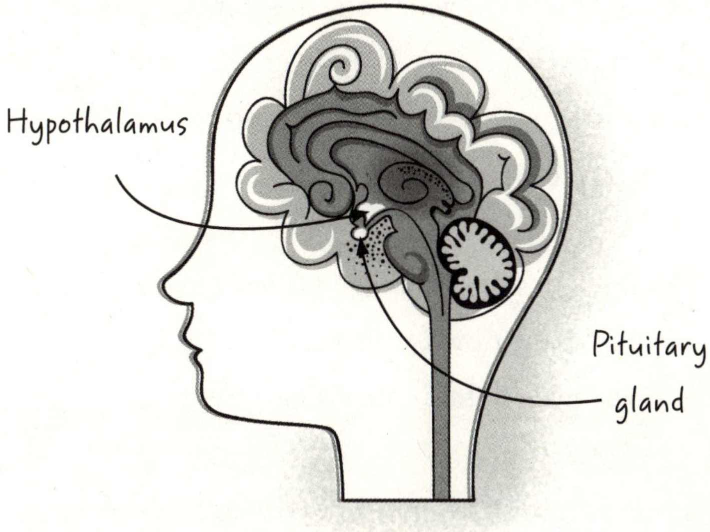

When the levels of GnRH are high enough, they give a signal to another part of your brain, called the pituitary gland, to release two more hormones called follicle stimulating hormone (FSH) and luteinizing hormone (LH).

FSH and LH travel through your blood to your ovaries (the parts of your body that contain eggs, or ova) and give a message to the eggs to start to develop. You can see where your ovaries are in the picture on page 40.

Your ovaries then start producing high levels of hormones of their own, called sex hormones, and this is when you'll start noticing big changes.

The main sex hormones in girls are called progesterone and oestrogen, though ovaries also produce low levels of the male sex hormone, testosterone.

The sex hormones help the ovaries to continue to develop and they also bring about changes such as getting breasts and starting periods (see chapters 6 and 8 for more about ovaries and periods).

"It's her hormones"

It can be annoying when adults say that everything you are feeling is down to your hormones, but it is thought that hormones can affect the way you feel. The strong hormones that make your body change during puberty may also make you feel moody and irritable at times. There's more about dealing with moods and feelings in chapter 15.

What triggers the trigger?

Scientists still don't know what causes the hypothalamus in your brain to start releasing the hormone that switches on puberty, but they do know this is starting earlier than it used to.

100 years ago most girls had their first period at 15; now most girls start around 12 or 13, but the average varies from country to country, person to person and place to place. Changes in eating habits may have something to do with it.

3. Bigger and taller

One of the first signs that you are on your puberty journey is that you put on extra weight and start to grow bigger and taller. Some girls go through a few growth jumps from about the age of 11, or have one big growth spurt. Some just grow gradually over several years.

- Your hands and feet get bigger first.
- Then your arms, legs and spine grow longer.
- Your thighs and bottom may get bigger.
- Your face gets longer and your voice gets a little lower.
- Your hips and shoulders get wider.
- Your muscles get stronger.

If you have a growth spurt early, you will finish growing earlier too. If you start later, you may catch up and even overtake your taller friends. Most girls have reached their adult height by about 15.

All of this growing is getting you ready for adult life and for a time in the future when you may choose to have a baby. The bones of your hips have to widen to make space for a baby to grow inside you and be born. The extra weight may be partly fat that you will eventually need for energy when you are pregnant and breast-feeding.

Some of the weight is because your bones, muscles, heart, lungs, and so on, are getting bigger and heavier inside you.

Did you know?

Your height increases twice as fast in the spring, but spring is the season when you are least likely to start your periods. Autumn is the season when you put on most weight.

Remember that putting on weight is normal and healthy before and during your teens as your body has to change from a girl's to a woman's.

Some girls feel happy with their new size and shape and glad they are growing up. Others may feel a bit self-conscious to start with, and this is natural too. Whatever your shape, it's important to eat healthily and to keep moving when you are growing (more about this in chapters 13 and 14).

Think tip

If you are feeling at all uncomfortable or worried about how your body is changing, tell yourself that your body is unique. It's good to share feelings with friends, but when and how you change is particular to you, so there's no point in comparing yourself to your friends – or anyone else.

4. Hair in new places

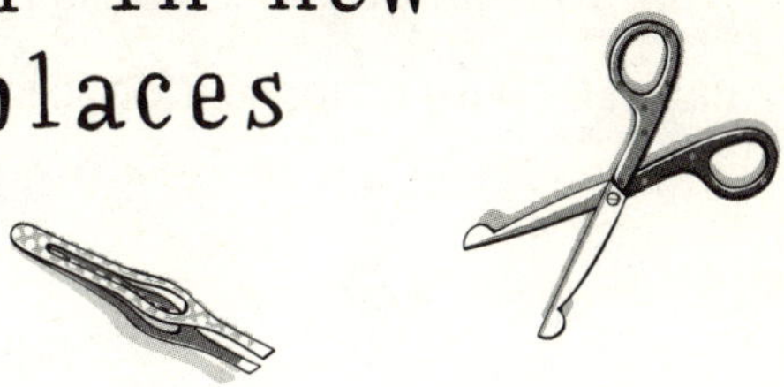

During puberty, another change you'll notice is that you start to grow hair in places where you didn't have it before. Hair that starts to grow between your legs and in a triangular shape at the front is called pubic hair, and it usually begins to grow at the same time as you first start to grow breasts. The hairs may be quite thin, straight and light at first but they usually get thicker and curlier and may darken as they grow. No one really knows why we have them.

Pubic hair doesn't keep on growing like the hair on your head. After about six months of growing, each hair falls out and a new one starts to grow in its place. If you find the hair gets so long and thick, it sticks out from your knickers or swimsuit, you can trim it carefully with round-ended scissors.

About a year later, you'll also start to sprout hair under your arms in your armpits, and the hairs on your legs, forearms (the lower parts of your arms) and even top lip may start to become more noticeable. Your body hair may be the same colour as the hair on your head or a different colour. Your underarm hair doesn't keep growing longer and longer but stops when it gets to a certain length.

All body hair is completely natural and there's no need to remove any of it if you don't want to. If you do choose to remove your underarm hair or the hair on your lower legs, think carefully about how you are going to do it. (You might want to ask your mum or an older female friend about whether she removes hers and ask for some advice.)

How to shave your legs and underarms

Shaving is a cheap and quick way to remove hair and for this you will need some soap, shaving foam or gel (from a supermarket or chemist) and a new disposable razor. (Don't be tempted to borrow a razor someone else has already used or is going to use.) It's easiest to shave your legs and underams in the bath:

- Squirt a blob of foam or gel onto one leg or cover it in soap and spread it over the hairs.
- Shave slowly and carefully from your ankle up towards your knee. You don't have to press hard.

- Remember to rinse the head of the razor in the water every so often.

- To shave under your arms, splash a little water in your armpits and apply soap, foam or gel. Shave downwards at first, then rinse the razor and finish by shaving upwards.

- Wash and dry your armpits and wait a few minutes before using deodorant, or it might sting a little.

Once you get used to it, shaving is quite easy, but the hairs will grow back fairly quickly, so you will have to do it regularly and you'll need a supply of razors as they go blunt with use.

Don't ever shave your face as the hair will grow back itchy and stubbly and look strange.

Other ways of removing hair

There are some other hair-removal methods which last longer than shaving:

- **Waxing** involves using strips of soft wax to pull the hairs out. It weakens the hair growth over time and works well, but it's best done by a professional beauty therapist so it can be expensive – and a bit painful. It may leave a rash for a few hours afterwards. As well as legs, some people get their 'bikini line' (the area at the top of their legs), armpits and facial hair waxed.

- **Epilators** are hand-held electrical devices that pull out several hairs at a time, in a way similar to waxing. You can buy rechargeable ones, ones with a cord, or ones with batteries. 'Wet and dry' epilators can be used with water.

- *Depilatories* are chemical hair removers which come as creams, lotions and foams. You can buy them in supermarkets and chemists, but make sure you get one designed for the area you want to remove hair from. You'll need to test the depilatory on a small patch of skin 48 hours before using it on a large area, to make sure you are not sensitive to the chemicals.

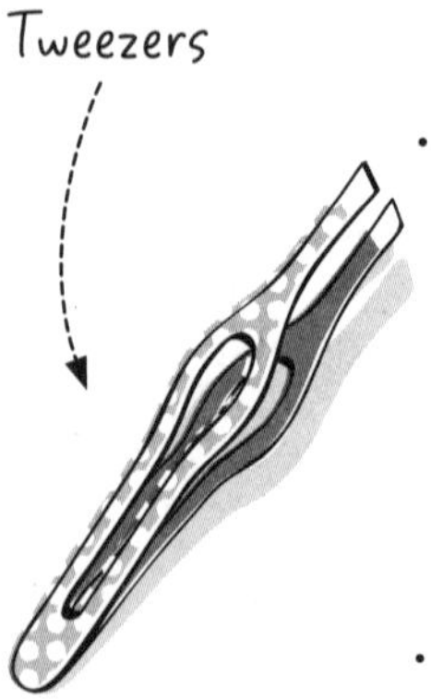

- *Tweezing or plucking* is pulling out individual hairs by hand with tweezers. It can be painful, so best only for single stray hairs and eyebrow hairs.

- *Bleaching creams* don't remove hairs but make them lighter and less noticeable if you have light skin. They are not really suitable for large areas, but can be used on your face. Buy a cream designed for the area you want to bleach, do a patch test 48 hours before and follow the instructions carefully.

5. Breasts and bras

Any time between the ages of about eight and 13, you may notice hard bumps behind your nipples. These are called breast buds and they mean that your breasts are beginning to grow. You'll also see your nipples sticking out more and the circles of skin around them (the areolas) getting darker and bigger.

For a while your nipples may feel a bit sore, tingly, itchy or achy, but don't worry, as this is normal. It's also quite common for one breast to grow faster than the other, but they usually even out in the end (though no one has perfectly symmetrical breasts).

Breasts grow slowly and if yours start growing when you are young, it doesn't mean they will be any bigger than other people's as they'll probably stop growing early too. If you start getting breasts later, they'll probably stop growing later too and may keep growing until you are 17 or 18. It can take as long as four years for breasts to grow to their adult size.

Many girls worry that their breasts are or will be too small, or too big or the 'wrong' shape. But despite all the attention breasts seem to get, there is no ideal shape or size. Like hands and feet, breasts come in all different shapes, sizes and colours:

- Petite
- Large
- Low
- Dark
- Pale
- Freckly
- Cone shaped
- Round

What are breasts for?

They can seem a bit annoying at first, but breasts are designed primarily for feeding babies, and many people think they look nice too. They are also sensitive to being touched. Breasts are mostly made of fat which protects the milk-making parts inside them. A woman's breasts can't start making milk until she's pregnant. When a baby feeds, the milk comes out of holes (too small to see) in the nipples.

Choosing and buying bras

It's really up to you when and if you wear a bra, and there are plenty of grown-ups who choose not to wear one for all sorts of reasons. The main reason to wear one is for comfort – to stop your breasts jiggling around in an uncomfortable way when you are running, exercising, dancing or playing sport.

The good news is that there are many styles to choose from at various prices. The bad news is that if they don't fit well, they can be uncomfortable. For this reason it's best to get measured in the bra section of a shop, or get a friend to measure you before you buy a bra. However embarrassing that may sound, it means you'll end up with a bra that is comfortable to wear (and you won't have to spend ages trying on different sizes until you find the right one).

Find your size

There are two parts to a bra size: the measurement around your chest, and the cup size. The smallest cup size is AA. A is a little bigger, then B, then C and so on, so a bra size might be 30A or 34C, for example.

The reason it's best for someone else to measure is because you should have your arms by your sides for measurements. This is how to calculate your bra size:

- Use a tape measure to measure tightly around your chest below your breasts. Add 12cm (5in) to this measurement to give your chest size.

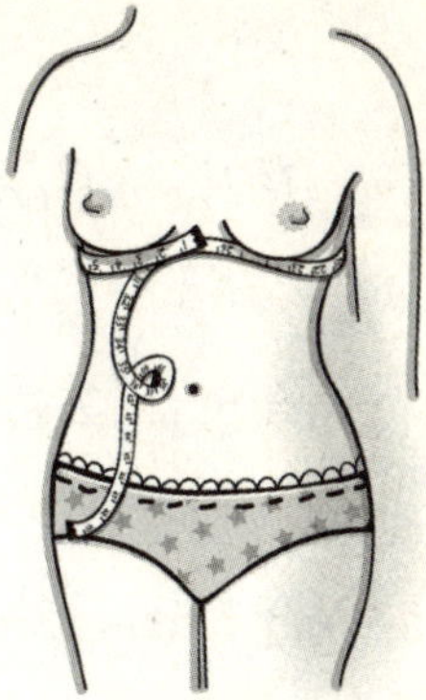

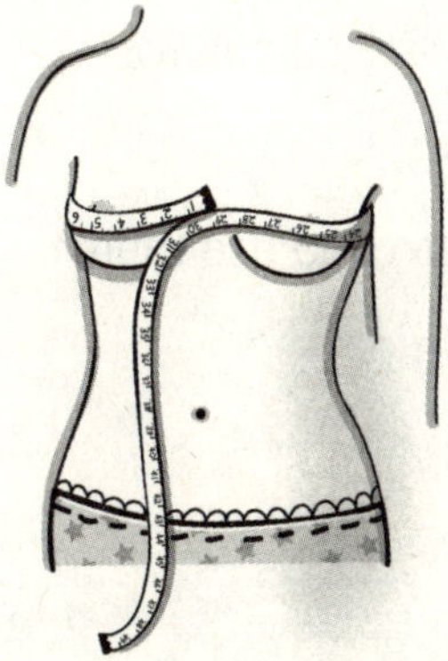

- Now measure loosely around your breasts with the tape going over your nipples, but not squashing them.

- If the second measurement is the same as your chest size, it makes you an AA cup.

- If there's a 1 – 1.5cm (½in) difference between the two numbers, you are an A cup.

- If the difference is 2.5cm (1in), you are a B cup.
- A 5cm (2in) difference makes you a C cup.
- A 7.5cm (3in) difference means you are a D cup.

You can also find international bra size calculators online (but you'll still need to know your measurements in inches or centimetres to use them). Go to **www.usborne.com/quicklinks** (see page 277) to find out more.

Think tip

The women who work in the bra sections of shops measure and advise people about bras every working day and have helped people of every imaginable age, shape and size. It's their job, so they'll be very used to people asking for help.

Choosing bras

Even if you know your size before you start bra shopping, it's still a good idea to try a few to see if you like the look and feel of them and check the fit before you buy one or more. (Remember: bras need washing.) Put your top back on over each bra to see if you're happy with the shape it gives you.

A bra should fit tightly around your ribcage, but not so tightly you can't breathe normally. If the cups are wrinkly, they are too big. If you bulge out of them, the cups are too small.

The straps should be comfortable on your shoulders and not so thin or tight that they dig in. You should be able to adjust the straps easily.

Which style and colour?

- The style you choose is up to you, but 'first' or 'teen' bras are soft and comfortable. (Bras don't have to be all frilly and lacy or hard to put on.)

- If you wear white shirts or t-shirts, it's best to buy white or pale-coloured bras to go underneath.

- If you do a lot of sport, it's a good idea to buy a sports bra too. Many girls prefer these (and not just for sport), because they are comfortable and you can put them on like a t-shirt.

- You may want to choose a bra that fastens at the front if you find the hooks at the back too fiddly.

- 'T-shirt bras' don't have seams on the cups and look best under t-shirts.

Breast checks

You might notice that your breasts become a bit swollen, tender or sore before your period (see page 73). This is normal, but once you've got breasts and have started your periods, it's important to get into the habit of checking them after each period for unusual lumps, bumps or any other changes. Stand in front of a mirror and use flat hands to do this. Go to **www.usborne.com/quicklinks** (see page 277) to see a demonstration. Look out for:

- Changes in the way the skin looks or feels, especially any dimpling, reddening or roughness.

- A lump or thickening in your breast that isn't usual for you.

- Unusual pain only in one breast.
- Liquid or anything coming out of the nipple (hairs and little spots around nipples are normal).
- Changes to the shape of the nipple, sores on the nipple or a different skin feeling.

The reason for these checks is to get to know what feels normal for you and to catch and treat any problems early. If you do notice anything unusual, even a lump, it's unlikely to be anything serious since breast disease is rare in teenagers. But you must still get it checked by your doctor, just in case.

Sadly, breast cancer is the most common cancer in adult women. It is also the principle cause of death from cancer among women globally. Detecting problems early could prevent many of these deaths.

6. What's going on inside me?

So your hormones are going into overdrive to make you start getting bigger, wider, heavier, taller, hairier, boobier, spottier and moodier. But what's going on inside you?

For your body to change into a woman's body, it has to get ready for having babies, and this means big changes to parts known as your sex organs. Most of these are hidden inside you so you won't even know these changes are going on until your periods start (see chapter 8).

Your inside sex organs are low down in your tummy, just above your bladder (the 'bag' which stores your urine) inside the bones of your pelvis. They consist of:

- Two ovaries
- Two fallopian tubes
- A womb (or uterus)
- A cervix
- A vagina

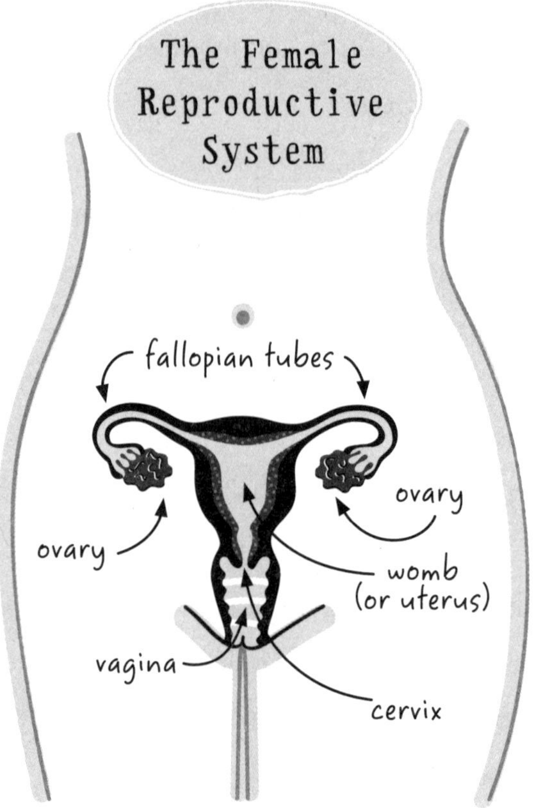

Your ovaries

are about the size and shape of small, whole shelled walnuts when they are fully developed. They are where your eggs, or ova, are stored and where sex hormones are produced. You are born with about half a million baby eggs in your ovaries, but it's not until you reach puberty that they start developing into mature eggs. One of these is released into a fallopian tube about once a month as part of your menstrual cycle (see page 54).

Your fallopian tubes

are a little shorter than pencils and about the same thickness when fully grown. When your hormones give a signal to one of your ovaries to release an egg, the end of one tube moves down and sucks it up and then starts to propel the egg towards your womb.

An egg may be fertilized if it meets a sperm (a 'seed' from a male partner) inside the fallopian tube when a couple have sex. If the egg reaches the womb and embeds itself in the lining, a pregnancy may begin. You can find out more about all of this in chapter 18.

Your womb or uterus

is where one day a baby may grow. Normally it's only about the size of your fist, but it will be able to stretch enormously. It has thick walls and lots of blood vessels in its lining. From puberty, about once a month, this lining gets thicker. If a fertilized egg doesn't embed itself in the lining, it starts to break down and flow out through your vagina. This is when you have a period. (There's lots more about this in chapters 8 and 9.)

Your cervix

(which means 'neck') is a narrow passageway that connects your womb and vagina. It's normally only the width of a pencil lead, but it will be able to expand to well over 50 times this width to let a baby pass through during childbirth.

Your vagina

is a muscular tube about 10cm (4in) long which connects your womb to the vaginal opening between your legs. It can also stretch to allow a baby to be born. Glands inside it produce a fluid which keeps your vagina clean and helps to protect it from infection.

Soooo...

. . . you think you know your bits from your boobs? To test your inside knowledge, choose the correct definition in the quick quiz which starts on the other side of this page.

Quick quiz

1. Vagina

a) A small tropical island

b) A bone in your foot

c) A muscular tube

d) A Roman goddess

2. Cervix

a) A female baby fox

b) A narrow passageway

c) A brand of glue

d) A character in French comics

3. Fallopian tube

a) What's inside a bicycle tyre

b) The underground train system of Fallopia

c) A medieval woodwind instrument

d) An organ connected to the uterus

4. Ovary

a) A Roman victory march

b) A covered walkway

c) A ceremonial robe worn by a priest

d) A place where eggs are stored

5. Womb

a) Another word for the uterus

b) An underground burial chamber

c) A small Australian animal

d) A jam-making society

Answers: 1.c 2.b 3.d 4.d 5.a

(But you knew that already, of course...)

7. On the outside

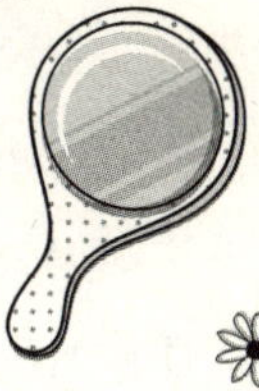

The sex organs on the outside of your body between your legs are known as your vulva – or, more usually, your genitals. They are not easy to see unless you use a mirror. Like the rest of our bodies, everyone's genitals are a little different in shape, size, colour and so on.

The **outer labia** ('labia' means 'lips') are two thick folds of skin which are normally closed over the inner parts of your vulva to protect them.

The lips of the **inner labia** are smaller and more sensitive to touch. They are not often exactly the same size or shape.

Your clitoris is a pea-sized lump under a little 'hood' where the inner labia meet at the front. It is the most sensitive part of your body.

Your vaginal opening leads to your vagina and other inside sex organs. It's where blood comes out when you have your period and eventually it can stretch enough to allow a baby to be born. It may be covered by a thin layer of skin called the hymen, though this wears away if you do a lot of sport when you are a child and it will disappear completely as your vagina grows.

It is normal and healthy for a little of the fluid which protects your vagina and keeps it clean to leak out through your vaginal opening sometimes.

Other bits

The little hole where your urine (pee) comes out is called your *urethra*. It's quite close to your vaginal opening but isn't part of your sex organs.

Your *anus* is the hole in your bottom at the end of your digestive system and is where faeces (poo) comes out.

What do you call it?

You may hear all kinds of words used for male and female genitals, some more pleasant or affectionate than others. While it's useful to know these words, there's never a reason to talk about parts of someone else's body in a way that sounds rude or crude (though you can call your own bits whatever you want...).

Did you know?

When babies first start growing inside the womb, boys and girls look identical until about 12 weeks into the pregnancy when their genitals start to look different. The part that becomes a clitoris if it's a girl develops into a penis if it's a boy. (You can find out more about how boys' bodies develop in Chapter 10.)

8. Starting your periods

Starting your periods is the biggest change that happens when you are growing up. When you have a period, some blood comes out of your vagina for a few days each month. This may seem strange at first and it can take a little while to get used to, but it's completely normal and a sign that your body is working properly.

You have periods because about once a month the lining of your womb starts to get thicker, filling up with blood and fluid to make a good place for a fertilized egg (one which has joined with a sperm) to develop into a baby. If the egg hasn't been fertilized by the time it reaches your womb from your ovaries (see page 41), this extra lining isn't needed, so it starts to break up and flow out through your vagina.

An egg can only be fertilized when a woman and man have sex (see chapter 18), but periods show that your body is working and that one day, when you choose to, you could have a baby.

When will it start?

Most girls start their periods sometime between the ages of nine and 15, but some begin earlier and a few start later. The average age is 13. Once you've started, you will have a period about once a month until the age you can no longer have babies (usually around 50) except during the time you are pregnant. From the time you start, this will happen 400 to 500 times.

For a few months before your first period, you may notice more fluid than usual coming out of your vagina. Another clue is that periods don't usually come along until at least two years after you start to grow breasts, so if you haven't got your first bra, you will probably have to wait a while. It's still a good idea to be prepared for when it does start so you know what will happen and what to do.

What will happen?

The blood from a period starts coming out slowly, so don't worry that you will feel a sudden gush. The first thing most people notice is a red-brown stain on their knickers when they go to the loo, or on their sheets or night clothes in the morning.

Some girls only bleed for a couple of days to start with. Others may have a heavier, longer flow of up to a week, but the most usual length for a period is four or five days. Even though it may seem that a lot of blood comes out, it will only be two or three tablespoonfuls over your whole period.

For the first few months, your periods may not come regularly (or come at all some months), but within a year or two, they will probably settle into a pattern. The whole pattern of hormonal changes, eggs being released from ovaries, the thickening of the womb lining and a period starting is called the menstrual cycle. Each cycle lasts about 28 days, but it can be shorter or longer.

Keeping track

You count your cycle from the first day of one period to the day before your next one starts. Once your periods are coming regularly, it's a good idea to keep a record on a calendar, or in your planner, organizer or diary so you know when to expect the next one.

Jan... Feb... Mar... April...

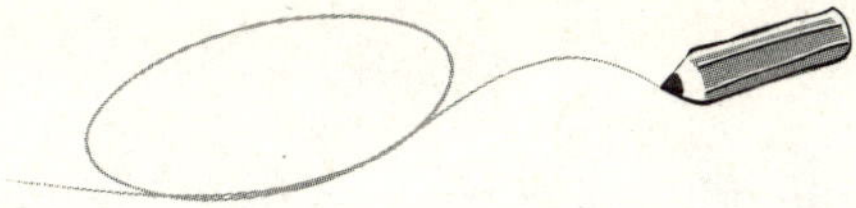

You can design your own special symbol, if you want, to mark when it should arrive (or just use a star, the letter 'P' or another letter).

What you will need

To soak up the blood from a period, most girls use sanitary pads (also called sanitary towels), or tampons. Tampons are tightly wound rolls of material which can absorb a lot of liquid. You can buy pads and tampons from supermarkets, chemists and online, in the section usually called 'Feminine hygiene' or 'Feminine care'. There are various different shapes, sizes and types. Pads collect the blood as it leaves your vagina and tampons fit inside it to soak up the blood.

It's up to you what you use, but you might find it useful to chat to an older friend, big sister, mum, carer, or another female adult you trust to find out what they use and to help you choose.

Pads

Pads are easy to use and should be comfortable to wear (and no one can see that you are wearing them). They come in a plastic wrapper and have a sticky strip on the back that you press onto the part of your knickers that goes between your legs. Some also have sticky flaps (often called 'wings') on the sides that fold over and stick onto the underneath of your knickers to keep the pad firmly in place.

The thickness of the pad you choose depends on how heavy your flow is. A thicker pad is often better for the first two or three days of your period when most of the blood comes out, and at night-time so you won't need to change it until the morning.

Pads may be described as 'regular' or 'normal' and 'super' and some are specially designed to use at night-time or are extra long. At the beginning, if you can, it may be best to try a few brands and sizes and see what works best for you. When your period is very light (for example at the end of your period or when you are expecting one to start) you can use a very thin pad called a panty liner.

During the day, you need to change your pad every few hours (or more often if your flow is heavy). Period blood is completely clean when it leaves your body, but once it comes into contact with bacteria in the air, after a while it may start to smell.

Tampons

The advantages of tampons are that they soak up period blood before it leaves your body and you can't feel them when they are inside. They are also useful if you like swimming as you can swim with one in.

There are two types of tampons. 'Applicator' tampons come inside a two-part disposable tube which helps you slide the tampon into your vagina; 'non-applicator' tampons just need to be unwrapped and pushed in gently using a clean finger.

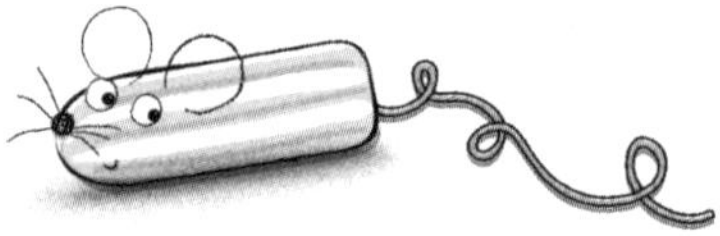

Both types have a string at one end which is securely attached to the tampon and allows you to remove it easily. Like pads, tampons come in different sizes and the size you need depends on how heavy your period is (not on your vagina size).

- Mini for when your flow is light
- Regular for medium flow
- Super or super-plus for heavy or very heavy flow

How to use tampons

It can take a bit of practice to feel confident using and changing tampons, but once you get used to it, they are easy to use and very comfortable.

It's easiest to start with non-applicator tampons and to practise putting one in when you are having your period and on a day when your flow is quite heavy. Inside each packet of tampons, you will find some instructions, but here's what you do:

- Start with a small size of tampon. Wash and dry your hands then remove the clear wrapper from the outside of the tampon and unfurl the string to make sure it is hanging down.

- Place the rounded top of the tampon (the end without the string) in your vaginal opening.

Look at the picture on page 40 if you are not sure where your vaginal opening is. You may find it easier to use the fingers of your other hand to hold it open.

- Relax as much as possible and try to make sure the muscles of your vagina aren't tense. Concentrate on breathing slowly and deeply for a few moments to help you do this.

- Push gently on the end of the tampon towards the lower curve of your back (not up towards your head) so that the tampon slides smoothly into your vagina.

- Keep pushing until the tampon is right inside you then remove your finger and wash your hands again.

Helpful tip

You might find it easiest at first to lie on your bed or on the floor with your knees up and your legs apart. With a bit of practice, you'll be able to change your tampon while sitting on the edge of the toilet or standing up with one foot on the toilet seat.

Once a tampon is inside you in the right place, only the string should be outside your body and you should not be able to feel the tampon at all.

If you get in a muddle, or the tampon doesn't go in all the way, just pull it out and try again with a new one. Never try to force a tampon into your vagina if it won't go in easily. It could be that you are a bit too tense or that the tampon is too big, so maybe go back to using a pad for a while and try again another time.

Removing tampons

You need to change your tampon *at least* every four hours (and for this reason, it's best to use a pad at night). To remove a tampon, wash your hands, sit on the edge of the toilet, or lie down with your knees up. Use one hand to find the string. Relax as much as you can, then pull gently and steadily down on the string to drag the tampon out. Dispose of the tampon and wash your hands again.

On 'heavy' days, you might need to change your tampon every couple of hours. When a tampon has absorbed as much as it can and is about to leak, you may feel a sort of bubbling inside your vagina, and, when you check, the string will have blood on it.

Always check you have taken out your last tampon at the end of your period.

FAQs about tampons

Does putting in a tampon for the first time hurt?

Putting in a tampon should never hurt if you are relaxed, the tampon is in the right place and the right size. If it's uncomfortable, it may not be in far enough. Take it out and try again with a new one.

Can a tampon get lost or travel up inside me?

No. Your cervix blocks the entrance to your womb and its opening is much too narrow to allow a tampon through.

Can a tampon fall out?

No. Tampons are held in place by the muscular walls of your vagina. Occasionally if you are straining to poo, you may push a tampon out at the same time. If this happens, just finish going to the toilet, wash your hands and put a new tampon in.

Do I have to remove a tampon to go to the toilet?

No. Your urine comes out of a hole called your urethra which is separate from your vagina. You can pee (and poo) as normal with a tampon inside you.

Can a tampon string break?

No. The string is strong and attached securely to the tampon. Occasionally it may curl up a bit, but you should be able to find it with a clean finger.

Will I still be a virgin if I use tampons?

Yes. A virgin is someone who has not had sex. It has nothing to do with using tampons.

Toxic shock syndrome

When your period is light, it's tempting to leave a tampon in for longer than four hours, to wear one all night, or to use a bigger size than you really need.

These are really not good ideas (in fact they are very bad ideas) as they increase the chance of developing a condition called toxic shock syndrome (TSS). This is a very rare, but serious bacterial infection.

Although it's very unlikely you will ever get toxic shock syndrome, if you do get two or more of these symptoms while wearing a tampon, remove it and see a doctor, or go to a hospital straight away:

- Sudden fever or high temperature over 39°C (102°F)
- Vomiting (being sick)
- Diarrhoea (watery poo)
- A rash that looks like sunburn
- Sore throat
- Dizziness
- Muscle pain and headache
- Confusion
- Fainting when you try to stand up

TSS doesn't just affect tampon-users and may seem like flu to begin with. If you have two or more of these symptoms, you need medical help, even if you don't use tampons.

What to do with used tampons and pads

Most public and school toilets have special bins for disposing of tampons and pads. (Signs may call them 'sanitary items' or 'sanitary products'). You may find it easiest to wrap a tampon in loo paper to dispose of it. You can wrap a pad in the wrapper from the next pad you are going to use, or just roll it up to throw it away.

If there isn't a special bin, put the wrapped pad or tampon in your bag or pocket (in a small plastic bag, if you have one) until you can find a rubbish bin to put it in.

Quick tip

Don't try to flush pads or tampons down the toilet because they can block pipes and are not good for the environment.

Eco-friendly and money-saving alternatives

During a woman's lifetime, she will use over 11,000 pads or tampons, all of which have to be paid for and then thrown away after use. It's estimated, for example, that in the US alone, 2 billion pads and 7 million tampons end up in landfill sites every year.

However, there are some re-usable alternatives available and if you do want to save money – and save the planet – some of these are available in chemists or you could track them down online:

- Natural sponges can be used instead of tampons and washed after use.

- Menstrual cups are soft foldable and washable silicone or rubber cups which fit tightly inside the vagina to collect the blood.

- Reusable, washable cotton pads fit inside a special leak-proof cloth pant liner.

9. Coping with periods

Periods are much easier to cope with if you are well prepared and know what to do if there are any problems. Since your periods may not have started or are not yet regular, it's a good idea to carry a little kit around in a small make-up bag so you are ready whenever your period starts. Here's what your period kit could include:

- Some tampons or pads.
- A small packet of wipes to clean up if you need to (though loo paper is fine).
- A spare pair of knickers in case of leaks.
- A couple of small plastic bags if you need them to dispose of pads or tampons or to keep stained knickers in until you can wash them.

Don't panic!

However well prepared you are, there will always be times when something goes wrong, but there is never any need to panic. If your period starts when you're not expecting it, or not prepared, use a tissue, paper towel or a wad of loo paper in your pants until you can get hold of what you need.

Women's toilets often have machines which sell tampons and pads, and remember that most women and older girls also have periods, so ask around your friends to borrow one. If you're at school, you should be able to get one from the school nurse or counsellor.

Some girls prefer to wear dark trousers or skirts when they are expecting their period and during the heavier days, just in case blood leaks through to their outer clothes. If you do get a stain on your clothes, you could tie your sweater or jacket around your waist to cover it until you can change or wash out the stain. If you're at a friend's house, you could ask to borrow something to wear.

If you get blood on your sheets, don't forget to tell your mum, dad or whoever is taking care of you. It's helpful if you take the sheet off and put it in the laundry or in some water to soak, rather than just leaving the stain to dry.

Top tip

If you have to handwash or soak knickers, clothes, sheets or towels because of a bloodstain, use cold water as hot water 'sets' blood and makes it harder to remove.

Period pain

Some girls go through years of having periods with few problems but some get pains called cramps, or a dull ache low down in their tummy or lower back, usually soon after their period starts. This is caused by the womb squeezing to try to help the blood trickle out. If you do get period pain, these ideas may help:

- Try gentle exercise, such as stretching or dancing.
- Hold a hot water bottle or warmed wheat bag against your tummy, or take a warm bath.
- Ask if you can have a painkiller (though if you need them all the time, you should see a doctor).
- Go to bed early and try to have a good sleep.

Pre-menstrual syndrome or PMS

This is the term for a collection of symptoms which can occur for a week or so before a period. They are thought to be caused by changes in hormone levels. PMS symptoms can include:

- Feeling grumpy, moody, miserable or irritable.
- Feeling tearful and lacking in energy.
- Having fuller, achy or tender breasts.
- Having a bloated tummy (because your body is retaining more fluid than usual).
- Getting spots on your face.
- Feeling headachy.
- Feeling restless.
- Wanting to eat lots of sweet, salty or carbohydrate-laden foods.

Coping with PMS

As with everything else to do with growing up, no two girls are the same, and while one may experience PMS every month, another may not recognize any of the symptoms. There's no complete cure for PMS yet, but if it does affect you, here are some things you could try:

- Eating healthy snacks (such as some nuts, a small sandwich, dried fruit or plain popcorn) between meals throughout the day.
- Taking some gentle exercise.
- Drinking plenty of water.
- Cutting down on salt.
- Cutting down on caffeine (in tea, coffee, energy drinks, cola and chocolate).
- Getting more sleep than usual.

Questions, questions, questions...

The best way to get answers to your questions about periods is to talk to your mum, carer or an older female friend, but here are a few more answers to some common questions about periods:

Can anyone tell I am having my period?

Not unless you tell them. If you wash every day and change your pad every few hours, there won't be any smell. The only way someone could see you were wearing a pad was if you wore skin-tight clothes. (Probably not the best choice during a period!)

Can I still exercise while I am having my period?

Yes. In fact light exercise such as walking, stretching, dancing or swimming can help relieve period pain.

Can I take a bath during a period?

Of course. A warm bath can be soothing if you have period pain and blood flows more slowly in water so you can take your tampon out before you get in. Use a wad of loo paper between your legs when you get out if you're worried about blood on your towel.

Do I need any special products to clean myself?

No. If you wash daily (including between your legs from front to back), change your pad or tampon regularly and wear clean knickers, you don't need any special products. Anything which says it is designed to help you 'stay fresh' or is described as 'intimate' is not necessary and can actually do more harm than good.

Do I need to take food supplements or extra vitamins?

Not if you eat a healthy and balanced diet (see chapter 13) though some teenage girls don't get enough iron to replace the small amount lost during a

Think tip

If you feel at all self-conscious about having your period and think people may notice, just take a look at all the women and girls around you next time you are out and about. Is there any way of telling who is having a period and who isn't?

period and this can make them feel tired. Iron can be found in wholegrain foods, almonds, walnuts, peanuts, dried apricots, prunes, green leafy vegetables, red meat, beans, lentils, shellfish, olives and eggs.

But see your doctor if...

Although having periods is completely natural and shows that you are healthy, there are times when you may need some medical advice. Here are some reasons to see your doctor:

- You get period pain that is so bad it seriously affects your life (you can't go to school or play sport, for example).
- You have severe symptoms of PMS every month.
- You are losing more blood than usual or there's so much blood your have to change your tampon or pad more than every two hours.
- After being regular, your periods stop for two months or more.

- You haven't had your first period by the age of 16.

- Your period lasts for more than seven days or less than three.

- You have little bleeds (known as 'spotting') between periods.

- You forget to take a tampon out and put another in and can't reach the first one.

- You have symptoms of toxic shock syndrome (see page 64). This is a medical emergency and you need to go straight to the doctor or a hospital.

- You have any unusual discharge from your vagina; soreness or stinging when you wee; itchiness, soreness or pain in your vagina or genitals.

10. What happens to boys?

Boys have to go through a lot of changes at puberty too, and, although it may not always be obvious, they also have worries and may feel self-conscious about how their bodies are changing.

Sexual development for boys can happen any time between ten and 18, but usually begins around 13 or 14. So that you know, here's a list of the changes that happen to boys' bodies. You'll see that some are the same as for girls.

- They get bigger, taller and more muscular.
- They put on weight.
- They sweat more.
- Their skin and hair become oilier and they may get spots.

- They get hairier and start to grow hair on their faces and (sometimes) chests and backs.
- They grow hair in their armpits and around their genitals.
- Their voices become deeper and may be squeaky for a while.
- Their Adam's apples (the lump at the front of the neck) stick out a little.
- Their genitals (penis and testicles) develop and grow bigger.
- They have more erections.
  (This is when the penis goes hard. Find out more on page 84.)
- They start making sperm and can ejaculate.
  (This is when sperm comes out of the penis. Find out more on page 85.)
- Their nipples may become painful and 'breasts' may swell up for a while.

How do boys' bodies work?

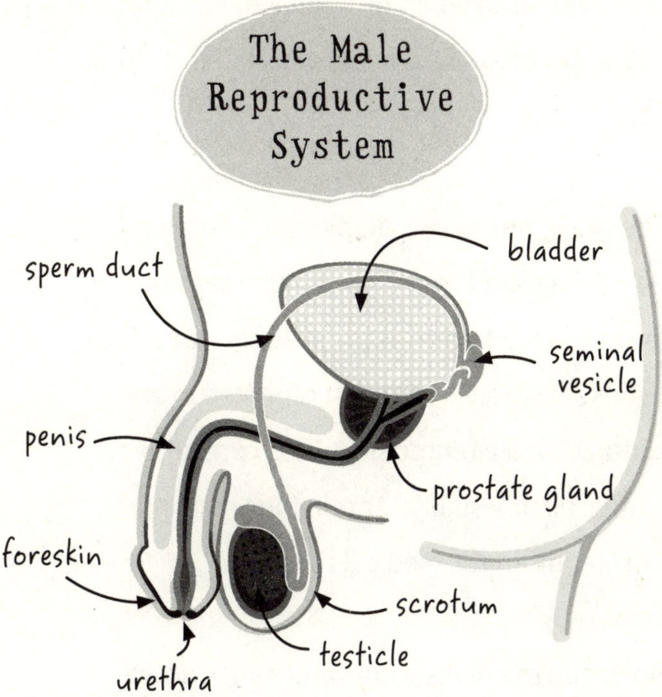

A boy has two *testicles* ('balls') where sperm (the male 'seeds' that can fertilize a female egg to make a baby) and male sex hormones are produced. Fully-grown, testicles are the size and shape of small plums.

The testicles hang outside a boy's body behind his penis in a bag of wrinkled, hairy skin called the *scrotum*. It is usually darker in colour than the rest of his skin.

The *penis* has two main parts, a *head*, or *glans*, and a *shaft*. The head is very sensitive. It is protected by a fold of skin called the *foreskin*. Some boys have their foreskin removed in an operation called circumcision. This can happen soon after birth, usually for religious reasons, or later in life, often for medical reasons.

Normally the penis is soft and hangs down, but when a boy is sexually excited, it fills with blood and gets bigger and stiffer and points upwards. This is called an erection. There are no muscles or bones in the penis.

Sperm reaches the penis by travelling along tubes called sperm ducts. On the way, the sperm are mixed with two fluids to make semen. These fluids come from the seminal vesicles and the prostate gland.

Semen leaves the penis through a hole at the end during ejaculation (also called 'coming'). Urine from the bladder also travels to this hole through the urethra, but muscles around the bladder ensure that urine and semen never come out of the penis at the same time.

What boys worry about

Despite not having to deal with periods or buying bras, puberty is not all plain sailing for boys, and they can get very anxious and embarrassed about the changes that happen as their bodies develop. These are some of their main worries:

My voice has gone weird

As a boy grows up, his larynx (voice box) gets bigger and this makes his voice deeper. While this is happening, for a while his voice may suddenly and unexpectedly go squeaky while he is speaking, and this can be embarrassing.

When will I need to shave?

Growing a beard and moustache is one of the last changes that happens to boys during puberty. Boys can feel self-conscious because the hair may be quite soft and patchy to begin with, or they may feel everyone else has started shaving and they haven't. Then they also have to learn how to shave their face without cutting themselves.

Am I big enough?

Boys may worry that they are not tall, broad and muscular enough, especially if friends develop before they do. Penis size and shape can also be a big worry and many young men convince themselves

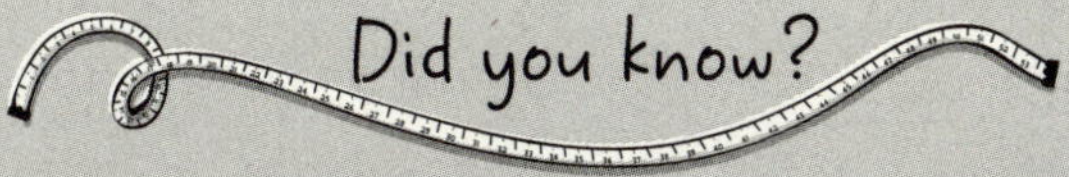

Did you know?

Adult penises are usually between 8.5cm and 10.5cm (3 and 4 inches) long when soft and 13cm and 18cm (5 and 7 inches) when erect.

that their penis is smaller than anyone else's, though this is unlikely to be the case. Like other parts of the human body, penises do vary and there's no 'right' shape as penises are all different, but erect penises are actually very similar in size.

I'm turning into a girl!

Some boys' nipples feel tender and small 'breasts' swell up during puberty, but once the hormones have settled down, these disappear. If boys don't know this is a normal part of puberty, it can make them anxious.

Everyone will see...

During puberty, boys often have erections at inconvenient moments, even when they are not thinking about anything to do with sex. Erections can come and go without warning and sometimes in embarrassing circumstances. It can be especially awkward if the erection won't go down.

I've wet the bed...

Most young men will at some point wake up to discover they have ejaculated in their sleep. It may be embarrassing to stain the sheets, but these 'wet dreams' are a completely normal part of growing up.

I keep losing it

Just like girls, boys may find that puberty is an emotional roller coaster ride as changes in hormone levels along with brain development cause rapid mood swings and sudden, angry flare-ups.

Am I smelly?

Quite possibly. Like girls, boys begin to sweat more during puberty and need to pay more attention to personal hygiene, including washing armpits, hair, genitals and feet, investing in a deodorant, brushing teeth and changing underwear regularly.

Will I ever be in a relationship?

That may well depend on the answer to the previous question . . .

11. Your skin and hair

If growing breasts and starting periods weren't enough, teenage girls also have to cope with some other side-effects of puberty such as greasy hair, outbreaks of spots, and sweating more. The good news is that there's plenty you can do to deal with all these things and stop them from making your life a misery.

What causes spots?

Whether you call them spots, zits, pimples or acne, outbreaks of these little red lumps are the bane of many teenagers' lives and can make you feel self-conscious. Spots are caused by the build-up of a type of oil called sebum. Your body produces sebum throughout your life and it seeps through tiny holes in your skin (called pores or hair follicles) to stop it from drying out. When you reach puberty, changes in your hormone levels can send sebum production into overdrive, and the extra oil sometimes blocks the holes, trapping bacteria and causing spots. This is just a normal part of being a teenager and has nothing to do with being dirty.

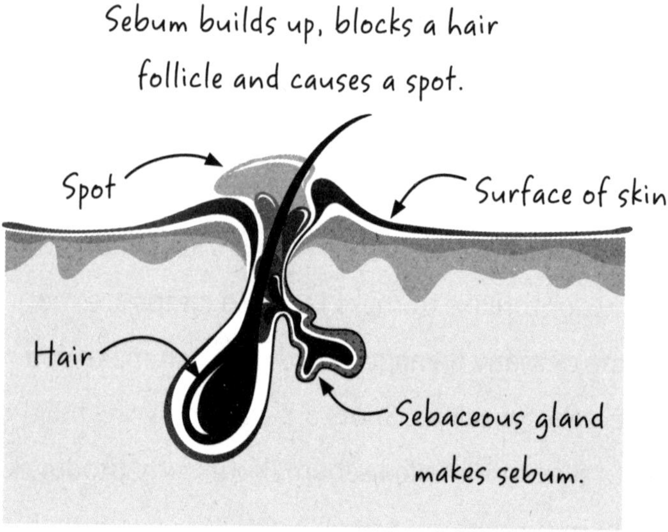

What can I do about spots?

Everyone seems to have their own remedy for spots, but here are some ideas that might help:

- Drink plenty of water and try to eat a healthy diet. (There's no evidence to suggest that eating lots of chips and chocolate gives you spots, but it probably doesn't help either.)

- Wash your face no more than twice a day with a facial wash or mild antiseptic soap designed for teenage skin. Use warm water and your hands (not a facecloth which can harbour germs).

- Try one of the spot treatments and cleansers you can buy from the chemists. Many people use ones that contain the antiseptic tea tree oil.

- Keep your hands and nails clean and try to avoid picking, playing with or repeatedly squeezing spots as this can make them worse and may also leave little scars.

- Keep your hair off your face and wash it often. (Lanky hair isn't a good look; it won't disguise spots and can make them worse.)

- If your spots are bad, ask if you can visit your GP for advice as there are plenty of treatments available (and they work).

Did you know?

Spots may get worse in the days before your period, but should start to get better once it starts.

To squeeze or not to squeeze?

Everyone will tell you not to squeeze your spots, but – in reality – most people can't resist. The reasons not to squeeze are that it can make spots bigger, redder, more painful, more infected and can cause little scars . . . but if you just must squeeze, here's how to do it safely (but maybe not right before a big party):

- Wash your hands well and use only your fingertips, not your nails, a needle or tweezers.
- Stop if nothing comes out, or if blood comes out.
- Blot the spot with a tissue or cotton pad, then dab an antiseptic such as tea tree oil on the area.
- Wash your hands - and leave your face alone to dry and heal.

Covering spots up

You may feel tempted to try to cover spots on your face with a thick layer of make-up, but this may just make matters worse in the long run as make-up can block pores and cause more spots. It's better to use a medicated concealer stick on small areas, but make sure it matches your skin tone really well.

In the past, many spot treatments didn't really work, but more recent ones do. If your spots are getting you down, don't suffer in silence. Visit your doctor and get some help.

Think tip

Nearly everyone has spots at some point in their lives, and most people (at least the ones worth bothering with) will be sympathetic and understanding when you have a outbreak.

Keeping clean

If you want to stay smelling sweet, you'll need to wash more often than you did when you were younger, and not just your face. This isn't because you are any dirtier but because you start to sweat more. Sweat is odour free when it forms, but when it comes into contact with the bacteria on your skin, before long it starts to smell.

You have sweat glands all over your body, but they are more concentrated in your armpits and around your genitals. For this reason, you'll need to shower, take a bath, or at least wash these areas every day (and after exercise) to stop any smells from developing. You'll also need to change your underwear, tops and socks more often than you did before.

Girly know-how

To avoid infection and irritation, always wash and dry your genitals from front to back using mild soap but no other products. Don't forget that the fluid from your vagina is natural and healthy, but if it gets itchy or sore, or smells bad, you may have an infection and need to see your doctor.

Deodorants

Using a deodorant in your armpits in the morning can stop your sweat from smelling all day. Some are combined with an anti-perspirant which stops you sweating so much. Experiment with different types and brands until you find one you like (within budget). You can use a roll-on or a spray, but remember that using a deodorant is no substitute for washing.

Top tips

Some deodorants can leave marks on your clothes – especially on dark tops. Look for ones which say 'invisible' to prevent this. If you do get a deodorant mark on your top while you're dressing, try rubbing it with a dry white sock to remove the mark.

Skin and sun

It's easy to think that a sun tan makes you look healthy, but it actually shows that your skin has been damaged by ultraviolet (UV) light from the sun. Sun damage can eventually lead to wrinkles and even skin cancer (the most common cancer in the 15 to 34 age-group). Tanning beds and sun lamps can expose you to even more harmful UV light than the sun does.

It's great to spend time outdoors in the sun, but it's important to use a sunscreen to keep your skin healthy. Sunscreens are given an SPF (sun protection factor) and the one you choose depends on your skin type (lighter skin needs a higher SPF).

Visit **www.usborne.com/quicklinks** (see page 277) to find out more about skin types and SPFs. Here is some advice to keep your skin healthy:

- Make sure your sunscreen covers both UVA and UVB rays.

- Always use a sunscreen of SPF 15 or higher.

- Reapply sunscreen after swimming, sweating and using a towel.

- Avoid spending too much time in the sun between 11 a.m. and 3 p.m. when the sun is strongest.

- Never let your skin burn in the sun - wear a hat and a top to protect your skin.

- If you really want a tan, you could try one from a bottle or can.

Piercing and tattoos

There's no legal age restriction on most body piercings in the UK, but you must be 18 or over to have a tattoo. To avoid infection or a botched job (that could scar you and make you very ill), it's vital that any piercing or tattooing is done by an experienced professional who uses sterilized equipment.

A tattoo applied with a needle is permanent so, if you're thinking about getting one, ask yourself if it would still look good when you are 60 . . . maybe a temporary tattoo would be a better idea for now?

Happy hair

Happily, there's a simple solution to greasy hair – just wash it more often and with a shampoo designed for greasy hair. If your hair is really oily, you may have to wash it every day and you could try washing and rinsing it twice each time. If your hair is long, just putting conditioner on the ends of your hair, rather than on your scalp, can help cut the grease. Try rinsing with lukewarm water too.

While you are going through the greasy hair stage, it might be an idea to avoid a style which needs loads of work to look good, or you may spend half your life attached to hair straighteners or a hair dryer.

Remember that too much heat can damage your hair and make it harder to care for in the long term. Try to find a style that works for you, not one that takes up all your time.

12. Teeth and nails

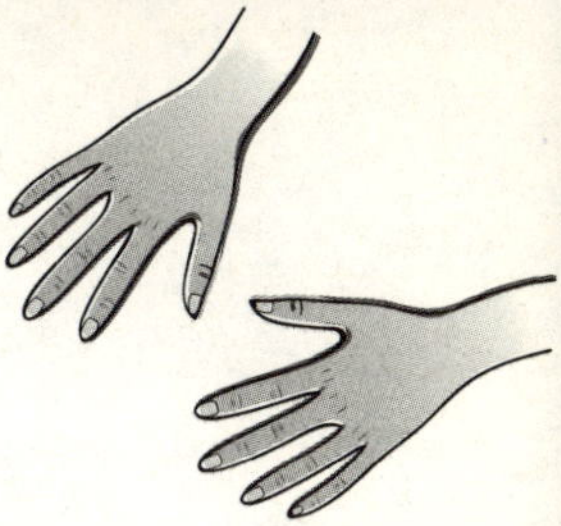

When you were younger, your mum, dad or carer probably trimmed your nails and made sure you cleaned your teeth every day, but now it's your job to take care of your nails and teeth. Getting into good habits now increases your chances of having problem-free teeth and nails when you are older.

The biggest causes of holes in teeth are thought to be sugary fizzy drinks and sweets, such as toffees, which can stick to teeth. So . . . (and how many times have you heard this?) to keep your teeth healthy, try to stick to water or milk instead of fizzy drinks and save sweets and other sugary things for special treats. Turn the page for more ways to keep your teeth and gums healthy:

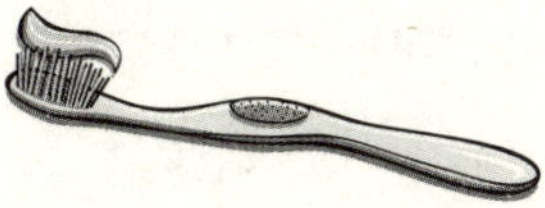

- Clean your teeth thoroughly using a toothbrush and toothpaste for two to three minutes every morning and every night.

- Replace your toothbrush every few months as the bristles start to get worn out.

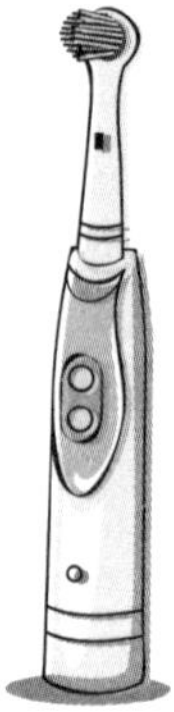

- Use dental floss or a little interdental brush between your teeth regularly to remove bits of food and bacteria that may get stuck there.

- Visit your dentist every six months for a check up.

About braces

Many girls and boys have to wear braces for a year or two to make sure their teeth grow straight and are lined up well. If you are one of them, though this may feel like a long time, remember that it's a big step to having nice teeth when you are older. Try to follow your orthodontist's advice about which foods and drinks to avoid and about how to clean your teeth and braces. You can look forward to the day when the braces finally come off and you can show off your perfect smile and easy-to-clean teeth.

Nail care

You don't have to spend a long time or a lot of money to keep your nails looking nice. Surprisingly, one of the best things you can do is eat a healthy diet.

Nails need iron, calcium, Vitamin B and potassium to stay healthy and these are found in cheese, milk, yogurt, bread, nuts and seeds, fruit and vegetables, red meat and beans. (You can find out more about healthy eating in the next chapter.) Turn the page for some more ideas to help you look after your nails:

- Trim your nails with nail scissors and file them often. File from the outside towards the centre of each nail. Make them all the same shape and length so they match each other.

- When you use hand cream, rub some around and on your nails too. Petroleum jelly, lip balm or olive oil can all be used to stop nails getting brittle.

- Clean under nails (dirty nails are not a good look) and trim toenails often too, cutting straight across.

- Use nail polish remover to remove varnish, not your nails or a nail file.

- Try not to bite your nails – this is a difficult habit to break, but you could try an anti-nail biting cream, liquid or polish that tastes really bad and reminds you not to nibble your nails.

13. Food and healthy eating

With all the changes your body has to go through during puberty, it's not surprising you need a good diet to stay healthy. (Your diet is the kinds of foods you usually eat, it's not about 'going on a diet'.)

Not only will eating the right kinds of food make you feel more energetic, it will make your hair, skin and nails look better and it can help you get to and stay at a weight that's right for you when you are an adult. Healthy eating really means eating the right mix of food in the right proportions and quantities. Here are the facts.

You need to eat different kinds of foods to get all the vitamins, minerals, energy and other things your body needs to stay healthy. Dieticians divide foods into five groups, and you need some of each:

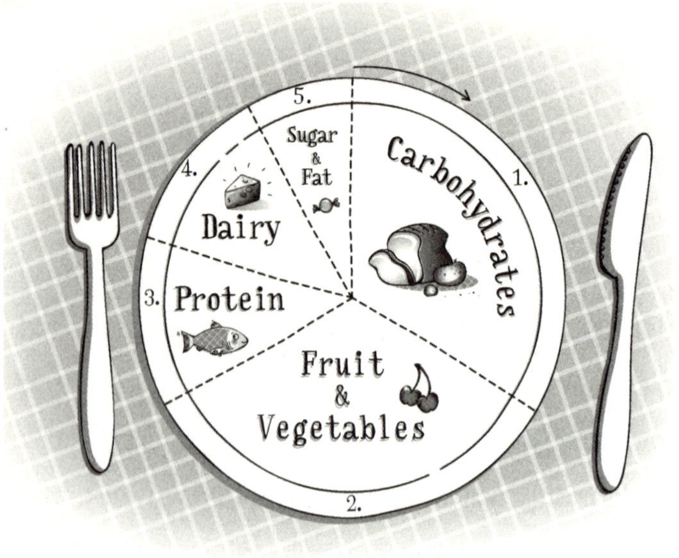

1. Bread, potatoes, rice, pasta, noodles and cereals

These 'starchy carbohydrates' give you energy, so you need plenty. They should make up about a third of all the food you eat.

2. Fruit and vegetables

These provide lots of important vitamins and minerals, as well as fibre, which keeps your digestive system healthy. You need at least five portions about the size of your fist a day.

3. Meat, fish, eggs, nuts, beans and lentils

All these foods are high in protein, which is essential for growth and you need two portions a day. A portion is a little smaller than a pack of playing cards (not a huge amount, in other words). This group also includes soya products such as tofu.

4. Milk, cheese, yogurt

These dairy products provide calcium which you need to develop strong bones and teeth, but you only need two portions a day – a portion is a glass of milk, a small piece of hard cheese (about half the size of a pack of cards) or a small pot of yogurt.

5. Foods high in fat and sugar

This group includes cakes, biscuits, crisps, chips, pastry, ice cream and a lot of 'junk' food. It's hard to describe portion sizes for fat and sugar as they are mostly hidden in other foods, but try not to eat too

many of these. You need some fat, but not a lot, and it should be mainly 'good' fat such as olive oil, corn oil, nut and seed oil and fish oil, rather than palm and coconut oil or animal fats such as butter and cream.

How much in total?

At puberty, you need to eat as much food as a grown-up woman because you are growing fast, but you also need to learn to 'listen' to your body. This sounds like a cliché, but it's true. Eat when you are hungry, give your stomach and brain time to register that you have eaten and only have more if you are still feeling hungry.

Because food tastes nice, it's very easy to eat more than you need (especially things which are not particularly good for you). Here are some more tips on healthy eating:

Leave yourself time to eat breakfast

After a night's sleep, your body and brain need fuel to get going properly. If you skip breakfast, you're more likely to crave sugary or salty snacks during the day and be less able to concentrate on whatever you need to do. Try porridge – it keeps you feeling full for a long time.

Eat regularly

That's three meals a day and some healthy snacks in between if you're hungry (fruit, nuts, a small amount of cheese or some plain popcorn). If you go too long without food, your blood sugar level drops and this can make you feel tired and grumpy.

Try to choose wholegrain foods

Choose wholemeal (brown) bread, wholemeal pasta, plain popcorn, brown rice, oats and wholegrain cereal when you can. These make you feel fuller for longer and can stop you from feeling moody. They are a good source of protein and vitamins and also fibre.

Avoid sugary, fizzy drinks

But drink at least six glasses of water a day – carry a bottle with you and refill it regularly.

Try to limit or cut out junk foods

This includes sweets and lollies, crisps, bought biscuits, burgers and chips – these usually contain lots of sugar, fat, or salt. They are fattening and they don't contain many nutrients.

Don't add salt to your food

You should have a maximum of 6g (less than ¼oz) or about a teaspoonful of salt a day, but most people get twice this just in the food they already eat, so you don't need to add more. Look for low-salt products such as canned vegetables if you help with shopping.

Eat fish

Fish is a good source of protein, vitamins and minerals and low in fat if you bake or grill it rather than fry it. Oily fish such as salmon, mackerel, sardines and herring contain Omega-3 fatty acids, which are thought to help combat diseases and skin problems. Some scientists say they help your brain to work well.

Eat five portions of fruit and veg a day

This includes fresh, frozen or canned food, and dried fruit such as raisins and apricots. Look out for food canned in juice or water with no added sugar. A glass of 100 per cent juice counts as one portion. Baked beans or other canned beans can count as one portion, but potatoes don't count because they are in the carbohydrate food group.

Here are some other things that count as one portion of fruit or vegetables:

1 apple, 1 banana, 1 pear, 1 orange, 1 nectarine, 2 plums, 2 satsumas, 2 kiwi fruits, 3 apricots, 6 lychees, 7 strawberries, 14 cherries, half a grapefruit, 1 big slice of melon, 1 large slice of pineapple, 4 heaped tablespoons of spinach, kale or green beans, 3 heaped tablespoons of carrots, peas or sweetcorn, 1 fruit smoothie . . . and a partridge in a pear tree (just joking about the last one).

Visit the Usborne Quicklinks Website (see page 277) for a full list.

Weight and eating problems

Puberty is a time when most girls start to worry about how they look and many think they are putting on too much weight. But it is also the time when you are meant to put on weight, especially on your stomach and hips, as your body changes. The keys to staying a healthy weight are to keep moving (some ideas in the next chapter) and to eat a healthy diet, following the tips in this chapter. There is usually no need to 'go on a diet'. In fact most people who go on a strict diet end up putting on weight.

It's easy to compare yourself with friends or with pictures of models and celebrities, but bodies come in all sorts of shapes and sizes all within the normal healthy range. Your weight depends a lot on your build and your genes as well as your diet. If you are seriously worried about your weight, talk to your school nurse, counsellor or your doctor. He or she can work out your body mass index (BMI) and give you advice about what you need to do if you are overweight for your age and height.

Think tip

The models you see in magazines are often unhealthily thin and have spent hours with make-up artists, hairdressers and clothes stylists to get ready. After that, their photos are nearly always digitally altered to make them seem perfect.

Comparing yourself with these 'fake' images might make you feel you are fat, even if your weight is normal for your age and height. Endlessly comparing yourself with other people won't help you learn to like your body; it will probably just make you feel unhappy. So try not to do it.

Good reasons NOT to 'go on a diet'

1. A strict diet could eventually make you put on weight – the body's natural response to thinking it is being starved is to store extra fat.

2. You need a whole variety of healthy foods and diets can mean you don't get all the nutrients you need.

3. It's boring – you can't really enjoy eating and it means you are thinking about food all the time instead of other things.

4. It won't make you look like whoever it is you want to look like, because you are not that person.

5. Girls who go on severe diets are 18 times more likely to develop serious illnesses known as eating disorders than those who don't.

Eating disorders

Worrying about food and eating can get out of control and begin to take over people's lives and make them feel very ill and unhappy. This can lead to illnesses called eating disorders. The most common kind is obesity (becoming unhealthily overweight) but there are some others too. Eating disorders are more common in girls than boys:

Anorexia nervosa

This often begins around the age of 14 or 15 and is when someone cuts down on food until they are actually starving themselves, but they still think they are fat. They may also become obsessed with exercise to try not to put on weight, even though they should still be growing, and to other people they look much too thin.

Side-effects of this serious illness include tiredness, stomach pains and headaches, hair loss, brittle nails and bones, extra hair growing on the body, stopping (or not starting) having periods, heart problems, and not developing properly.

Bulimia nervosa

This eating disorder is more common than anorexia, but usually more hidden. It often starts in the late teens or early twenties and it is when someone gets into a cycle of binge eating (eating far too much) and then feeling guilty and making themselves throw up, or using laxatives (medicines that make you poo) to 'purge' the food from their bodies.

Side-effects of bulimia include stomach problems, damaged teeth (from the acid brought up from the stomach) and heart problems.

Binge eating and comfort eating

This is when someone uses food to deal with difficult emotions or to comfort themselves when under stress or worried. They eat far too much, but don't purge the food and so are often overweight. This puts them at risk of suffering diabetes, high blood pressure and other serious conditions. Binge eaters often do so in private because they feel ashamed of the amount they eat and of feeling out of control.

Help for eating disorders

If you think that you, a friend or family member has or is developing an eating disorder, it's vital to get help. It's easier to recover if treatment starts early. Talk to an adult you trust, such as a parent, teacher, school nurse or counsellor, or your GP. Find out more at **www. usborne.com/quicklinks** (see page 277).

14. Keeping moving

Yes, you've heard it before, but exercise really is very good for you, especially during puberty. This is the time you need to build up strong bones and muscles and get into habits which will help you to stay healthy when you are older. In case you are not entirely convinced, here's a list of some of the many benefits of regular exercise:

- Exercise reduces body fat and so helps control your weight and makes you look good.
- It makes you feel more energetic, physically and mentally.
- It makes you feel good and can improve your self-confidence.

- Exercise helps you fight worry, anxiety and stress.
- It can lift your mood and helps prevent depression.
- It helps you sleep.
- It reduces the risk of you developing major illnesses such as heart disease, diabetes and some cancers by 50 per cent as you get older.

- It aids co-ordination, balance and flexibility and improves your stamina.
- It helps you build strong bones and muscles, including your heart.
- It can help you develop mental and social skills such as planning strategy, working with others, and thinking ahead.

How much exercise do I need?

To get fit, you need to do some sort of exercise for at least an hour a day to develop stamina, suppleness and strength. This sounds like a lot, but it can be split into chunks and it includes PE at school, fast walking, bike riding, dancing, or playing games in the park (if you like doing that kind of thing).

If you've been fairly inactive for a while, build up slowly and steadily, setting yourself realistic goals.

The most important thing is to find out what you enjoy and vary your activities so you don't get bored. You don't have to join a gym (although many do welcome younger teenagers) or be the school sports star to enjoy exercise.

Two or three times a week, you need to do some vigorous activity such as sport or fast running that makes you breathe much harder and faster and increases your heart rate (so that you can't say more than a few words without pausing for breath).

Here are some exercise ideas:

- Fast walking (to school or with a dog perhaps).
- Energetic dancing (try one of the interactive screen games that show you the moves).

- Swimming, cycling, football, trampolining, gymnastics, tennis, badminton, volleyball, rollerblading, ice skating, martial arts, skipping with a rope, running, horse riding, basketball, netball, rounders, baseball, softball, kayaking, yoga, paintballing, streetdance, boxing, archery, bowling, fencing, table tennis, circuit training . . .

Top tip

Make notes in a diary to keep track of how much you are moving each week. If you are not getting enough exercise, build up week by week until you hit the target.

Monday: walked Mollie – 30 mins. Played dance game with Nina – 20 mins.

Tuesday: netball at school – 40 mins. Swimming with Mum and Ben – 30 mins.

Get off your bottom!

Some recent studies have shown that sitting or lying down for long periods is bad for your health. Spending hours watching television or playing computer games and not moving is thought to increase your risk of many diseases as you get older, even if you are active for an hour each day. It's difficult to avoid sitting but, if you can, you could try screen games that let you play sports or dance, go for a 'real' walk or bike ride, or even help with chores around your home – mowing the lawn counts as exercise!

Sleep

Sleep is as important as food and exercise, especially for teenage brains and bodies, but most teenagers do not get enough. Not getting enough sleep can limit your ability to learn, concentrate and solve problems; it can make you more prone to spots; make you eat too much and make you feel cranky. Sleep is especially crucial for teenagers because it's while you're snoozing that your brain reorganizes itself. It's also when your body releases a hormone essential for your growth spurt, so sleep patterns can even affect your height.

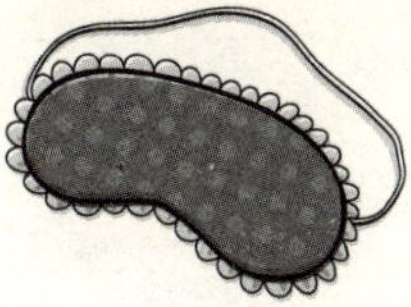

How much sleep do I need?

11 to 15 year olds need just over nine hours sleep a night, but this can be hard when your body clock tells you to stay up late when you still need to get up early. If you find it hard to relax and drift off, try these tips:

- Make sure bedtime really is bedtime – ban your phone, tablet or laptop from your bedroom so you're not tempted to stay up late playing games, social networking or chatting with friends.

- If worrying about things you have to do keeps you awake, make a list in a notebook or diary. Then you can forget about them until the morning.

- Avoid watching television in the hour before it's time to sleep. Try taking a shower or bath, or drawing or reading instead.

- Don't eat, drink or exercise just before bedtime and don't leave homework until the last minute. Your brain and body need time to wind down.

- Tempting as it is, try to avoid long lie-ins at weekends and in the holidays as these can disrupt your sleep patterns.

Did you know?

A school in the US delayed the start of classes to give teenagers some extra time in bed and for breakfast and noticed a significant improvement in the performance of its students.

15. Your moods and feelings

One minute your mum seems the most understanding person on the planet; the next, everything she does fills you with rage. You feel happy and full of energy one moment and miserable and tearful the next. You find yourself snapping at your best friend and tiny little things can suddenly make you feel really irritated. Does any of this sound familiar?

If so, you are perfectly normal and you are not alone. Your teenage years are a time of deep emotional changes which can sometimes be uncomfortable as well as exciting. You don't want to feel and act like this; you're not a nasty person and you're not going mad, but when you are going through puberty, mood swings and extreme feelings can be hard to predict, hard to understand, and even harder to control.

Brain changes

Extreme emotions happen because, as well as the changes going on in your body – triggered by hormones – your brain is in the process of undergoing massive changes too.

The part of your brain responsible for your emotions develops before the part that is responsible for things such as planning, decision-making and understanding the emotions of others. So it's no surprise that teenagers have strong feelings, but sometimes find it hard to think things through, or understand the effect their behaviour has on others.

While your brain is 'rewiring' it can make you feel moody, irritable, disorganized, confused, angry, anxious and even depressed or aggressive at times.

New connections - use them or lose them

Brain changes, along with hormonal changes, can really affect the way you feel about things, and sometimes moods change so quickly, it's hard to keep up. But try not to despair; your hormones will settle down eventually. And while your brain is rewiring it's a very good time to pick up new skills such as learning to play an instrument or to speak a new language.

In fact, brain researchers believe that the connections you use in your brain during your teenage years become 'hard wired' into your adult brain, while others die off. So if you don't use connections that help you learn a new language, for example, this skill will be much harder, or impossible, when you are older.

Dealing with difficult feelings

Not all emotions come out of the blue. Sometimes there are good reasons why you feel like you do when you've had a fight with your best friend, an argument with your sister, or something has gone wrong at school or in a relationship.

Everyone feels moody, angry, jealous, frustrated, embarrassed, hurt, sad, rejected, let down, knocked back, picked on or left out from time to time. But you can learn ways to cope with and manage difficult feelings (and it does get easier with practice). First of all, here are some things that don't work:

Suppressing or bottling up feelings – locking feelings away inside you, trying to bury them, remove them from your thoughts or holding them in can only

make you feel under greater pressure until you may 'explode'.

Withdrawing – hiding away from everybody, sulking and refusing to speak can make you feel helpless and even depressed.

Dumping feelings – blaming other people for the way you feel and handing responsibility for your feelings over to them. ("It's all your fault that . . .")

'Acting out' – being taken over by your feelings, so that you start shouting, swearing, slamming doors, hitting out or breaking things, for example.

Here are some tactics you could try instead:

- Let off steam in a safe way – hit your pillow, go for a fast walk or run, dance to loud music. Cry if you want to.
- Take some deep breaths and give yourself time to acknowledge and think about what you are feeling and why ("I'm feeling really angry because...").
- Talk to someone you trust. It's amazing how just airing and sharing feelings can help you feel better and the other person might have ideas for how to resolve or improve the situation.

- Write down how you feel in a journal, notebook or diary; write a song or poem or make a piece of art to try to express your feelings.

- Think of what you could do to make things better and make yourself feel better. If you need to confront someone about their behaviour or apologize to someone about yours, it's better to do it when you are calmer.

- Try to focus on some good things in your life – What are you looking forward to? What do you like doing? What are you good at? What don't you have to worry about?

- Try to eat well and get a good night's sleep. Things may seem less important or easier to cope with in the morning when you have calmed down, are not so tired and have a clearer head.

- Let the feelings go... when you have taken notice of feelings and understood why they're there, you may be able to let them go.

Worries and anxieties

It's normal to feel frightened or worried from time to time, but if someone worries about things too much and this stops them from enjoying life, they may be suffering from anxiety.

All sorts of things can cause anxiety – worrying a lot about what other people think of you; upsetting experiences such as parents being ill; parents arguing a lot or separating; losing someone close to you; a frightening experience happening to you or someone close to you; problems at school; exams looming, or a new experience such as moving home, moving country or changing schools.

Anxiety can cause all kinds of physical symptoms including:

Faster breathing and heartbeat, breathlessness, trembling and sweating, needing to rush to the loo all the time, feeling sick in your stomach, not being able to concentrate on anything, feeling unable to move or talk, disturbed sleep or difficulty sleeping.

Coping with worry and anxiety

Big things that make life difficult and cause worry and anxiety are often out of your control, but there are things that you can do to make them affect you less. If you feel your worries are getting out of hand, here are some things you could try to make yourself feel better:

Think about whether you are really picking up on someone else's worries, rather than the worries being yours. Anxiety often runs in families, so you may be worrying because someone in your family is worried (and that person's worries aren't actually yours).

Talk to someone about how you feel. You will need extra support in difficult times so you might also need to talk to someone you trust outside your family, such as a school counsellor, a teacher, your head of year, youth worker, a family friend or school nurse.

Try to give yourself more time to get used to changes that happen at home or at school. No one feels instantly comfortable with new experiences and in new situations and you may need longer than other people to get used to them.

Spend more time doing the things you enjoy and are good at. This may be something you do at school, an after-school or lunchtime activity such as music or drama, swimming, a sport, or a club that you go to with friends.

Learn yoga or meditation, or try one of the relaxation techniques on the next two pages.

Breathing relaxation technique

Try this if you're feeling nervous or panicky or when stress, shock, anger or anxiety make you start breathing with quick, shallow breaths and you can feel your heart beating faster than usual:

1. Find somewhere comfortable to sit down if you can.
2. Put one hand on your stomach to check how fast you are breathing.
3. If you're taking a breath every couple of seconds, make yourself take a deep breath in and start counting in your head.
4. Breathe out slowly through your mouth while you count slowly to five.
5. Take a deep breath in and breathe out again counting slowly to five.
6. Carry on doing this until you are breathing in and out naturally.

1... 2... 3... 4...

Relaxation routine

You can do this sitting or lying down somewhere quiet and comfortable.

1. Close your eyes and breathe slowly and deeply.
2. Think about any areas of tension in your body and try to relax those muscles.
3. Imagine all the tension leaving your body.
4. Focus on each part of your body in turn, starting with your head and neck and working down your body. Think of warmth and heaviness as you let each part relax completely.
5. After 15 to 20 minutes, take some deep breaths, stand up slowly and stretch.

If you have tried these ways of helping yourself and still don't feel better, you need to see your doctor who can discuss treatment and may refer you to a specialist.

Moody or depressed?

Nearly everyone, children and teenagers as well as adults, occasionally feels sad or low for all kinds of reasons. Feeling miserable is a natural reaction to upsetting or stressful experiences. But when these feelings go on and on and begin to take over someone's life, it can become an illness called depression.

Depression affects about five in every 100 teenagers and is more common in girls than boys. You are more at risk of becoming depressed if you think you have no one to share worries with and are under a lot of stress. But depression is usually caused by a combination of events and experiences, not by just one thing.

How do I know if I have depression?

If you have most of the symptoms in the list below and have had them for a while, it could mean that you are depressed:

- Feeling miserable and unhappy and 'empty' or 'numb' inside.
- Feeling lonely most of the time.
- Losing interest in and not enjoying things you used to like.
- Becoming withdrawn – avoiding your friends, family and your usual activities.
- Feeling moody and irritable so you are easily upset and often tearful.
- Finding it hard to concentrate and finish things.
- Not taking care of yourself and your appearance.
- Feeling tired and lacking in energy.
- Sleeping too much or too little.

- Feeling bad or guilty; criticizing, blaming and hating yourself.
- Having frequent mild health problems such as headaches or stomach aches.
- Having your appetite change.
- Thinking about death and wanting to die.

Getting help

Depression is a common and treatable illness, but it can be hard to ask for help and talk about how you feel when you are suffering from it. It's vital that you do ask for help though, especially if you are having suicidal thoughts (thinking about dying), not taking care of yourself, or harming yourself.

Talking to someone you trust and who you think will be understanding is the first step, but you may also need professional help from your doctor or a counsellor to start getting better.

For sources of help and to find out more about anxiety, depression and other mental health problems such as bipolar disorder and schizophrenia, go to **www.usborne.com/quicklinks** (see page 277). If you suffer from exam stress, there are some ideas to help you cope in chapter 22.

Did you know?

Four out of ten teenagers say they have felt so miserable that they have cried and have wanted to get away from everybody and everything.

One in five teenagers sometimes thinks that life does not seem worth living.

For the majority of people, depression and other mental health problems are only temporary and can be treated.

Anti-misery toolkit

Here are some ideas for ways to cheer yourself up if you're feeling fed-up for whatever reason:

- List in your head five things that you like about yourself. (If you can't, ask someone else to.)
- Write down five things that make you happy.
- Look at some photos of times when you felt happy.
- Distract yourself with a film that makes you laugh.
- Listen to some favourite music (though nothing too miserable) and sing along.

- Go for a walk or a run, jump on a trampoline, dance, or do something else active.
- Phone a good friend for a chat.

- Take a long, warm bubble bath.
- Talk about how you're feeling with someone you trust.
- Write, draw, doodle, play music or cook something.
- Do something you are good at and enjoy.
- Cuddle up with a blanket or one of your old toys and read a favourite book.
- Play a silly game with some friends.
- Declutter and rearrange an area of your room.

16. Feeling confident

When things around you are changing, your hormones are working overtime and your brain is being refurbished, it's very easy to lose confidence in yourself and start to feel all sorts of doubts about your abilities, the way you look, your relationships, and who you really are.

Girls tend to blame themselves and find fault with themselves quite easily and may find that the confidence they had when they were younger starts to trickle away. Lack of confidence can make you feel awkward, embarrassed and self-conscious and can lead you to think that you come from the weirdest family on Earth. It can make you unable to resist pressure from other people to try things you really don't want to or don't feel ready to do.

Lack of confidence can make you feel that you just don't fit in and that no one will ever find you attractive. It can convince you that everyone else is cooler, cleverer and more popular than you are.

So how do you learn to fight these feelings? There are no instant answers, but some of these ideas can help:

Confidence think tips

Tell yourself you don't have to be perfect (nobody is...).

Tell yourself you don't have to be good at everything (nobody is...).

Try to be proud of what you are good at (whatever it is) and aim to get even better at it.

Try not to compare yourself with others all the time. (They don't have your life, your family, your genes, your hair, your talents or your favourite sweatshirt...)

Don't be too critical of yourself when you make a mistake – that's how you learn.

Congratulate yourself when you do something well (even if no one else does).

Find what you enjoy doing and what interests you (even if other people find it strange).

Try to find others who share your interests. Joining a drama, debating or sports group are all good ways to learn to boost your confidence.

Tell yourself it doesn't matter if someone doesn't like you. (Not everyone has to like you and you don't have to like everyone.)

More confidence think tips

Don't spend time with people who mock or say mean things about you (on the internet or in 'real life').

Don't mock or say mean things about other people.

Do spend time with people who make you feel good, who support you and appreciate you for who you are.

Practise standing up tall and straight, looking people in the eye when you talk to them, taking a deep breath and saying what you want to say calmly and clearly.

Develop your own taste and style in EVERYTHING. (You don't have to like the same music, wear the same clothes, eat the same food, watch the same films, do the same things or hang out in the same places as anyone else if you don't want to.)

Try new things (though it's not a good idea to apply this to drinking, smoking, drugs, unsafe sex or other things that could harm you).

... and a word about drinking

Try NOT to believe that drinking will make you more confident. It may make you less inhibited, but then you might make some very bad choices – or throw up, or fall over, or pass out . . .

How confidence helps you

If you learn to feel confident, you don't need to criticize, judge or put other people down to feel better about yourself. It also means you don't have to spend all your time worrying about what other people think of you, or comparing yourself with others, or trying hard to be seen as popular and fashionable. And you don't feel you have to give in to peer pressure – going along with things just because other people do.

Being confident doesn't mean you are boastful or that you think you are better than other people. You still understand that the world doesn't revolve around you. But you know that you have as much right to be heard and to be happy as anyone else.

When you are confident you feel happy being yourself; you value yourself and your talents and abilities, whatever they are, and you don't feel you need to be perfect all the time. Most of all, when you are confident, you can make choices that are right for you. Worth spending a bit of time learning to be confident?

For more ideas on how to gain confidence in yourself, go to the Usborne Quicklinks Website (see page 277).

Gaining body confidence

Because the media is full of images of seemingly happy and 'perfect' girls and women (often all of a similar age, height and body type), it's very easy for girls to get sucked into the idea that their life would be better if only they could change their body in some way.

At the same time, girls are fed the idea that they always have to compete with other girls to be conventionally beautiful, at whatever cost, and whatever their natural shape, size, height, age or skin colour.

If you're feeling under pressure to change the way you look, try to remember you are not in a beauty competition and being good-looking is NOT the same as being happy or successful in life. In fact psychologists have found that people who are considered conventionally beautiful are just as likely to feel unhappy (or happy) as anyone else.

There are many different kinds of beauty, so try to find the kind that means something to you, and try not to look to the unrealistic (and often digitally altered) images shown in magazines, adverts, websites, blogs, social networking sites and so on to tell you what is attractive or unattractive.

Top tip

People who are involved in sport or take regular exercise tend to have more body confidence than those who don't, as they value what their bodies can do, not just what they look like.

A word about ‘boob jobs’

Some of the women who show off their breasts on the internet or in magazines have had plastic surgery to change their shape. Plastic surgery may involve putting sealed sacs of silicone inside the breasts to make them bigger or a different shape. Mostly women have this done because they think it will improve their appearance, but sometimes it is done for medical reasons, for example after women have to have a breast removed because of cancer.

These artificial breasts can lead girls to think that ‘plastic’ breasts are somehow normal and compare them with their own. But if, in the future, you ever find yourself considering a ‘boob job’, think long and hard. These are just a few of the many problems associated with breast implant surgery:

- Infection (bacteria can be released from the implant into the body).
- Chronic pain (severe pain that doesn't go away).
- Breast or nipple numbness.
- Scar tissue.
- Hardened and misshapen breasts.
- Breakage and leakage of implants.
- Dissatisfaction with how the breasts look.
- Implants masking symptoms of breast diseases.
- Difficulty breast-feeding a baby.

It's usual to become a bit obsessed with how you look in your teenage years, and it's tempting to think that plastic surgery might make you feel better about yourself. But remember that, as well as being very expensive, this surgery can be dangerous. Many women end up having to have further surgery to remove implants, and almost half experience problems or need more surgery as they are not happy with the results.

17. Relationships

The biggest change in your feelings that usually happens as you go through puberty is that you start to have exciting feelings that you haven't had before and begin to fancy other people. When you were younger, you may have had boys as friends, but now you may begin to notice them in different ways.

When you see a person you fancy, you get funny, warm, fluttery feelings inside. This is because you are physically attracted to them. You may think about them all the time, even when they are not there, and you try to find ways to get them to notice and speak to you (though, if they do, you may suddenly feel flustered and do or say something silly that you didn't mean). All these feelings are normal, but they can be confusing and a little scary as well as exciting.

Crush or love?

You can fancy or 'have a crush on' someone who doesn't even know you exist, such as a celebrity or actor, or it might be someone you know at school, a friend's brother or even a teacher. Your feelings during a crush may be strong and passionate, but they don't usually last longer than a few weeks, and sometimes less. You might decide to tell your friends about your feelings, or you may prefer to keep them a secret.

Not all girls find they fancy or have a crush on boys. When you are growing up, it's not unusual to fancy another girl. You might then go on to date boys later, or you might have relationships with girls and women all your life. Some people fancy girls and boys. Finding out who you are attracted to (discovering your sexual orientation) is part of growing up. Find out more about sexuality on pages 171 to 175.

Not all crushes are one-sided. It could be that the person you have a crush on fancies you too, and when you find this out, it feels great. If one of you then plucks up the courage to ask the other one out, and you get on well and you like their personality, you might decide to be in a relationship. You may even feel you are in love. But what happens then?

Is it a good relationship?

In ALL your friendships and relationships, it's very important to know if the relationship is a good, or positive one or a bad one. In a positive and caring relationship, two people take time to find out about each other, respect each other and they feel good about themselves and each other (most of the time).

Turn the page for a checklist of the kind of things that good relationships include.

Some features of a good relationship

- Having fun and laughing together.
- Having things in common.
- Trusting each other.
- Being good friends.
- Respecting each other's opinions.
- Being able to disagree with each other.
- Being able to talk about it when you have had an argument.
- Making decisions together.
- Having time and space to see other friends when you want to.
- Having your own interests.
- Being able to go at your own pace in the relationship (including sexually).
- Feeling safe.
- Feeling confident.

Think tip

In a relationship, it's easy to get so bound up in trying to please the other person that you forget what makes you unique and special. Remember that the whole point of relationships is to choose someone who likes and respects you for who you are, and not just to feel grateful because someone has shown some interest in you.

Bad relationships

In a negative or bad relationship, one person dominates and controls the other. They may get angry and jealous if you talk to other people; call you names to make you feel bad; threaten you physically or emotionally; pressurize you to do things you don't want to do or don't feel ready to do, or post unpleasant or revealing things about you on the internet.

If you recognize any of these things in a relationship, it's time to end it (even if you think you are in love). Go to the Usborne Quicklinks Website (see page 277) to find sources of support to help you do this.

If you really are not sure about whether you and your partner get on, try the quiz on the facing page.

Now look at the answers at the bottom of this page. If your answers truthfully matched these, then the relationship might be going somewhere and is worth continuing with.

If not . . . really sorry, but it's time to break up. Turn the next page for some advice.

1. YES, 2. YES, 3. NO, 4. NO, 5. NO

Quick quiz

Answer 'YES' or 'NO' to these questions to find out more about your relationship:

1. Can you relax, laugh and have fun together most of the time?

2. Does your partner give you support when you are feeling unsure of yourself or unhappy?

3. Does your partner look at you as if you're mad when you talk about your feelings and worries?

4. Do they ever make nasty comments about you around other people or online?

5. Do they ever pressurize you into doing things you don't want to do?

Break-ups

Sometimes relationships aren't especially negative; they just don't work out for all sorts of reasons. Sometimes two people just aren't 'compatible' (they just don't fit together and can't get on). It takes two people to make a relationship work, and if one person doesn't want that then the relationship needs to end.

If you have been through a break-up, it feels hurtful and sad, but you need to remember that it does not mean there is anything wrong with you; it's just that your ex was not the right person for you.

If you are the one being 'dumped', try to keep your dignity (though you can weep and wail as much as you like later in private) and try not to wallow in self-pity (at least not in public). You could try some of the 'dealing with difficult feelings' tips on pages 134 to 135.

The painful feelings will fade with time, but in the meantime you should be able to fall back on your family and friends and the things you enjoy doing to make yourself feel better. Give yourself a few weeks to get over it and don't feel you have to rush into another relationship just to feel that someone wants you.

Rejecting other people

If someone asks you out and you're not interested, it's best to tell them simply and in as kind and direct a way as you can. It takes courage to ask someone out, and no one deserves to be ridiculed or made to feel bad for doing so.

You could say something along the lines of "Thanks very much for asking, but I am seeing someone else at the moment." Or "That's nice of you, and I'd like to be friends, but I want to stay single at the moment/but I'm afraid I don't feel the same way." Try not to give false hope by suggesting it might happen another time or by agreeing to go on a date when you know you are not interested.

If you feel you need to tell someone a relationship has to end, try to do it respectfully and be brave enough to do it face to face and in private. No one should ever be dumped by text, email, letter, over the internet or with other people around. Explain why you are breaking up, but talk about how you are feeling, rather than blaming the other person or making them feel bad.

Don't expect that you will instantly become friends again after a break-up. It takes time to get over feelings of hurt and rejection and to feel comfortable in the same space as someone you have rejected or who has rejected you.

Staying single

Some girls enjoy being single and don't have a partner until after they leave school; others start worrying if they are single the moment they reach puberty. Teenagers often feel under such pressure to be in a relationship, they end up going out with the wrong person just so they can say they have a partner.

Being in a bad relationship is much, much worse than being single and there's absolutely no reason to go out with anyone unless you really like them, they like and respect you for who you are, and they make you feel good.

There are also all sorts of advantages to staying single for longer. Turn the page for some examples:

Benefits of being single

Having more time to focus on other things in life such as schoolwork, sports and interests.

Having fun girly nights with your friends.

Doing what you want to do without having to worry about another person.

Being able to spend time finding out who you really get on well with.

Having time to get to know yourself and what makes you happy.

Sexuality

Like your brain and body, your sexuality develops and may change during your life. When you are finding out about yours, it's important to take your time and to remember that people have the right to express and explore their sexuality in a way that's right for them. Your sexuality is an essential part of who you are, and it's up to you to discover it, not for other people to decide or 'diagnose' it.

You don't choose your sexual orientation (whether you are straight, lesbian, bisexual, etc.) any more than you choose the size of your feet or height. It is just the way you are and part of what makes you unique. Nobody can 'turn' you gay or straight. Some girls know from quite an early age that they are only attracted to other girls. Others

Did you know?

Surveys show that at least five per cent of children grow up to be gay or lesbian.

Many gay people say that they first knew they were gay at primary school.

find they fancy both girls and boys and experiment to find out what their preferences are. A lot of people (including adults) are unsure what their sexual orientation is. Just so you know, here are some different terms associated with sexual orientation:

Asexual - If someone is asexual, they don't feel sexually attracted or respond sexually to anyone.

Bisexual, or bi - A bisexual person is emotionally and sexually attracted to both men and women, but not necessarily at the same time.

Celibate - A person who is celibate chooses not to have sex.

Heterosexual (straight) - A heterosexual person is emotionally and sexually attracted to the opposite sex (that is a woman to men and a man to women).

Homosexual (gay or lesbian) - A homosexual person is emotionally and sexually attracted to people of the same sex. A gay woman (often known as a lesbian) is attracted to women; a gay man to men.

Transgender - Transgender people have a strong feeling that their gender identity (their sense of being male or female) is not the same as the physical characteristics they were born with. A transgender person can be straight, gay, lesbian or bisexual. Some want to be the opposite gender and have surgery and take hormones to change their bodies.

Transvestite - A person who (sometimes) likes to wear clothes usually thought of as belonging to the opposite sex. This doesn't necessarily mean they want to become another gender and they can be straight, gay, lesbian or bisexual.

Coming out

Coming out is when someone chooses to tell other people that they are lesbian, gay, bisexual or transgender. This is a personal decision and should be a positive one. But many young people fear it will affect the way their friends and family feel about them and worry especially what their parents' reaction will be.

Some heterosexual parents may just assume that their children will be heterosexual too, so it can come as a shock when they find out their teenager is gay or bisexual. But many parents accept their child's sexuality and are very supportive and reassuring.

In reality, people who love you and are real friends will be supportive and respectful whatever

Think tip

If someone reacts badly when they find out that you are not heterosexual, remind yourself that the problem does not lie with you, but with the other person's ignorance and fear of difference.

your sexual orientation is, and if ever you are feeling confused and uncertain about it. If you feel yours aren't, or need support in coming out, there are groups and organizations you can turn to for help. Go to **www.usborne.com/quicklinks** (see page 277) for sources of advice.

Meeting other young people who are going through a similar experience is essential to help you overcome any feelings of isolation and anxiety.

Homophobic bullying

Hating, abusing or bullying people because they are gay or bisexual causes huge amounts of misery and suffering, but more than half the lesbian, gay and bisexual students in UK schools say they have experienced this at some time. Homophobic bullying includes pushing, hitting, name-calling, teasing or tormenting someone, or deliberately making them feel stupid or uncomfortable (online as well as face to face) because of their sexual orientation.

If you know this is going on, or if you are being bullied, tell someone you trust – a parent or carer, your teacher, your doctor or the police, or call a helpline (see page 259) but don't ignore it.

If you are the bully or have got caught up in bullying, you have a serious problem and need to talk to someone about it – urgently.

18. Sex... and all that stuff

You start to become a sexual person when your hormone levels change and your sex organs begin to develop, but this usually happens a long time before you are ready to have sex with someone. People have sex or 'make love' mainly because it can feel very good, especially with someone they feel deeply about, are attracted to and are in love with.

People also have sex when they want to have a baby, but you can just as easily get pregnant when you don't want a baby, if you have sex without using contraception (see chapter 19).

If you don't have 'safer sex' (sex using a condom) you also run the risk of getting, or passing on, one of the diseases known as sexually transmitted infections (or STIs). More about all of this in the next chapter.

What is sex?

You probably know all this already, but just in case you weren't paying attention that day. . .

When people talk about 'having sex' they usually mean when a man puts his penis (willy) inside a woman's vagina. This is also known (in medical language) as sexual intercourse or (in everyday language) as 'going all the way', 'hooking up', 'doing it', 'going to bed with someone' or 'sleeping with someone' (because most sex happens in a bedroom on a bed).

There are many, many other phrases and words you will hear people using to describe sex, and there are all sorts of other ways people enjoy being sexual with each other without actually 'having sex' in this way.

For the penis-in-vagina type of sex to happen, a couple kiss, cuddle, touch each other and get very close until they both become sexually excited, or aroused. The man's penis gets stiffer and the woman's vagina releases some slippery fluid. The man slides his penis carefully into the woman's vagina and then moves it a little way in and out rhythmically until he has an orgasm, which is a rush of intense sexual pleasure. During orgasm (often also called 'coming' or 'cumming') he ejaculates. This is when a small amount of a liquid called semen comes out of the man's penis.

Semen contains hundreds of millions of sperm and (if the couple are not using contraception) the sperm can swim up the woman's body and into her fallopian tubes, where one of them may meet an egg from her ovaries. The sperm enters the egg and fertilizes it. If the fertilized egg then implants itself in the wall of the woman's uterus, a pregnancy begins.

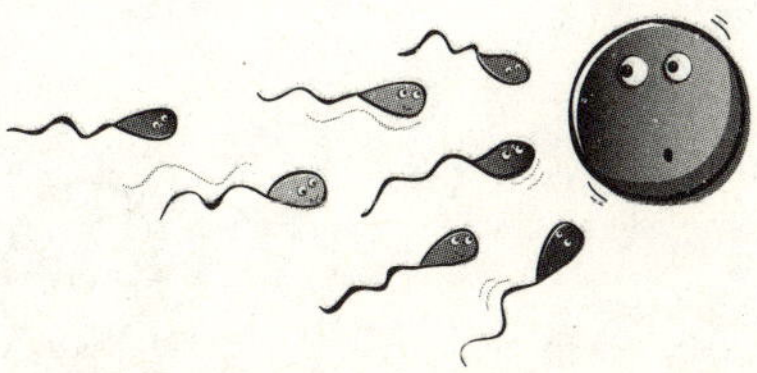

Take your time

So those are the facts. But even when you know what this kind of 'having sex' is, know how to stop babies by using contraception and know how to protect yourself against STIs (more information in the next chapter about all this), it doesn't mean you have to do it or are ready to do it. For sex to be enjoyable and safe, you need to be ready mentally and emotionally as well as physically.

As your body starts to change, you may find you have sexual thoughts and feelings and start to feel physically attracted to other people. These thoughts can pop into your head at odd times, day or night, and you might find yourself fantasizing about being with the person you fancy. This is quite normal and a safe way of exploring your feelings.

Once they start having sexual feelings, most people become curious about their own body and may start to masturbate to find out what physical sexual feelings are like. Masturbation (often called 'wanking') is when you touch your own genitals because it feels good. Most girls touch and rub their clitoris, which is the most sensitive part of their body, and may become so aroused they have an orgasm, which is an intense tingly, pleasurable feeling in the genitals, which makes your whole body feel very relaxed.

Masturbation is very safe as you can't catch a disease or get pregnant from it. It is also a good way to get to know your own body's responses. If you know what makes you feel good, when you do come to have sex with another person, you can let your partner know too.

If you are physically attracted to someone and in a good relationship, there are all kinds of ways to express sexual feelings without 'going all the way', as long as you both feel comfortable doing them. You can hold hands, laugh, flirt, kiss, hug, cuddle, kiss using tongues (French kiss) and touch, fondle, stroke and rub each other, for example.

How do I know if I am ready?

If you are in a good relationship and thinking about having sex with your partner, there are lots of questions you need to ask yourself to find out if you really are ready. As you get older, it can seem as if everyone else has had sex (or at least *says* they have), but this is absolutely no reason to have sex yourself. No one should ever be pressurized into having sex just because their partner wants to, or because they know other girls have done it. So make sure you can honestly answer 'yes' to ALL these questions:

- Do you really want to have sex (for you, not for someone else)?
- Do you like, trust and respect your partner?
- Are you comfortable with all the physical things you have done so far with your partner?
- Are you sure your partner has never tried to get you to do something you weren't comfortable with?
- Do you both know how to take responsibility for safer sex?
- Do you have and know how to use condoms?
- Are you relaxed enough around your partner that you can tell them to stop if you change your mind or you're not enjoying it?
- Can you make your partner understand that 'no' means 'no'?

Did you know?

It is against the law for anyone to have sex with a young person under the age of 16. This is known as 'the age of consent'. This is the same for men and women and for heterosexual (straight) and homosexual (gay/lesbian) sex.

Some bad reasons to have sex

- Because the other person wants to.
- Because you want to make someone like you more.
- Because you're too drunk to stop it from happening.
- Because you have taken drugs.
- Because you are too scared or shy to say 'no'.
- Because you are afraid your partner will break up with you if you don't.
- Because you don't want to be a virgin.

- Because you are afraid your partner will do it with someone else if you don't.
- Because you want to get back at parents who disapprove of your partner.
- Because you want to rebel against your parents who disapprove of you having sex.
- Because your friends say they are doing it.
- Because you want to make someone jealous.
- Because you want to get it over with.
- Because you want to find out what it feels like.
- Because you like kissing and touching and think this means you have to keep going.
- Because you've done it before so you might as well do it again.
- Because someone says they will give you money or a gift if you do.
- Because someone pressurizes you or threatens you.
- Because you think having a baby will make your partner stay with you forever.

Did you know?

A recent survey found that a third of 15 to 19 year old girls regretted having sex that happened after they had been drinking.

It's always your choice

In spite of all the boasting, most young teenagers are NOT having sex. Surveys show that the average age when people first have sex is about 17, but you're not at all unusual if you want to wait until you're older, as many people do. It should always be your decision to have sex (or not to have sex), so don't do it before you're with the right person, know how to use contraception, and know you're ready. Teenagers often find that changing a relationship into a sexual one is a bigger step than they imagine, so don't ever be pushed into something you don't want or don't feel ready for.

FAQs about sex

Does having sex hurt?

It doesn't usually hurt, though some people feel a small amount of pain when a penis first goes into their vagina. It can hurt if the boy puts his penis in too suddenly, or if you haven't had enough time to get aroused and so your vagina is dry. (See page 203 to find out about safe lubricants you could use).

You should be able to trust your partner enough to tell him what feels comfortable and how to take things slowly and comfortably.

How long does it take?

The actual 'in and out' bit may only take a few seconds or a few minutes, which can be disappointing for you if that's all you do. But if a boy knows how to slow down so that you both have an enjoyable time, there will be plenty of kissing, touching, licking and playing (called 'foreplay') before and after this bit, so it can take much longer. That's one of the reasons why it's important to be able to trust and communicate well with your partner, before, during and after sex.

What is oral sex?

Oral sex is kissing, sucking and licking each other's genitals. Some people enjoy it but others aren't interested or don't like it. When a girl does it to a boy it is called a 'blow job'.

Can a boy pee inside a girl by mistake during sex?

No. The penis is designed either to ejaculate or to urinate (pee). It can't do both at the same time.

Do women have orgasms during sex?

They may or may not. It doesn't most often happen just through penetrative (penis-in-vagina type) sex, as the clitoris doesn't get enough stimulation. Often women show or tell their partners what to do to help them get excited (though not all sex has to involve orgasms for either partner).

Can you get pregnant the first time you have sex?

Yes. You can get pregnant any time you have penetrative sex and in any position, even if this happens before your periods have started. The only way not to get pregnant is to use a condom, or another form of contraception correctly . . . see the next chapter.

19. Protecting yourself

If you do decide that you want to, and are ready to have sex, it's vital to protect yourself both from pregnancy and STIs (sexually transmitted infections) such as HIV and chlamydia.

To protect yourself from pregnancy, you need to use a reliable form of contraception.

Contraception (also known as 'birth control') is a wonderful thing and more than 60 per cent of women in the world use it. In the days before effective methods were easily available, women often lived in fear of unwanted pregnancy, or resigned themselves to having baby after baby until they were worn out. This is often still the case in places where women do not have access to contraception or can't use it for religious or cultural reasons.

Contraception allows a couple to prevent pregnancy when they have sex, and there are many different methods. All methods, apart from male condoms, are used by women, which leads some people to assume that contraception is a woman's responsibility. But, in a relationship, it is something you should both be responsible for.

No method of contraception is 100 per cent effective, but, if used correctly, the methods described in this chapter prevent pregnancy 95 to 99 per cent of the time. There are lots of myths about avoiding pregnancy, so remember that . . .

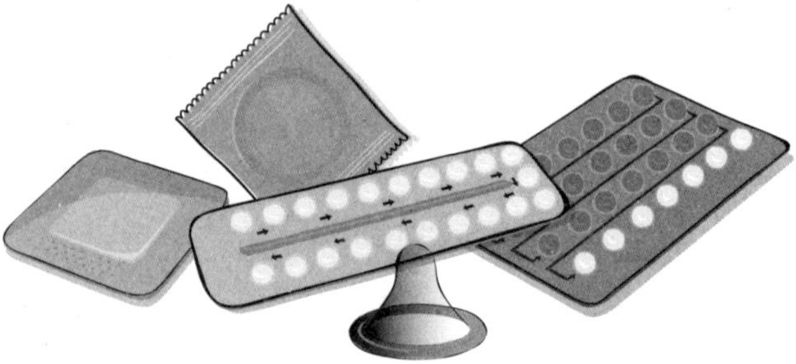

. . . a girl or woman CAN get pregnant:

- The first time she has sex.
- When she is having her period.
- Before she has started having periods.
- Whatever position the couple use for sex.
- Wherever the couple have sex.
- If she does not have an orgasm.
- If the man withdraws (pulls out) of her vagina before he ejaculates (comes).
- If the man doesn't go all the way in.

Quick quiz

Which of these can prevent pregnancy?

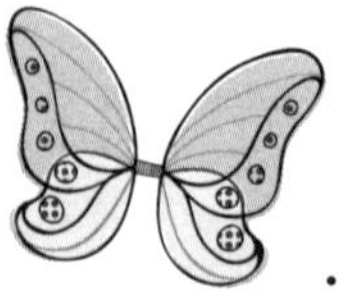

- Being drunk
- Having sex standing up
- Having sex with the woman on top
- Having sex in a shower or swimming pool
- Jumping up and down immediately after sex
- Taking a bath, or peeing immediately after sex
- Pushing on your tummy button after sex
- Sneezing for at least 15 minutes after sex
- Using cling film or a plastic bag instead of a condom when you have sex
- Squirting water into your vagina after sex
- Wearing a tiara and fairy wings when you have sex

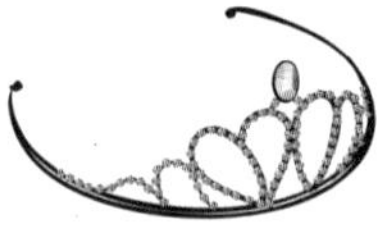

Answer

The answer, of course, is NONE OF THEM.

The only way for a male and female couple to avoid pregnancy is for them not to have the kind of sex where sperm can come into contact with the woman's vagina.

Or for them not to have sex at all.

Or for them to use a reliable contraceptive method when they have sex.

Did you know?

Every year in the UK, over 7,000 girls under the age of 16 become pregnant.

Methods of contraception

Method	What is it?	How effective?
Male condom	A very thin latex or plastic cover that is put on a man's stiff penis before it goes into the woman's vagina to collect the sperm when the man ejaculates.	98% if used correctly
Female condom	A soft, thin plastic bag that loosely lines the vagina and covers the area just outside it to catch sperm when a man ejaculates.	95%
Contraceptive vaginal ring	A small, flexible plastic ring put inside the vagina to release hormones which prevent pregnancy	Over 99%
Contraceptive pill (also called 'the pill')	A pill that contains hormones that prevent pregnancy.	Over 99%
Diaphragm (also called 'the cap') with spermicide	A flexible latex dome, used with a cream or jelly called spermicide and put into the vagina to cover the cervix and prevent sperm being able to travel.	92 to 96%
Contraceptive patch	A small patch stuck to the skin that releases hormones to prevent pregnancy.	Over 99%

Pros	Cons
Easily available, cheap or free, and also the best way to protect against STIs (sexually transmitted infections) as well as pregnancy.	May split or come off if not used correctly. Can't be re-used.
Protects against STIs as well as pregnancy.	Not as widely available as male condoms. Can't be re-used.
One ring can stay in for three weeks, so you don't have to think about contraception every day.	You must know how to insert and remove it correctly and be comfortable doing so. Not as easily available as condoms. **Doesn't protect against STIs.**
May also reduce bleeding, period pain and pre-menstrual symptoms.	Must be taken daily. Forgetting to take pills, vomiting or diarrhoea can make it less effective. **Doesn't protect against STIs.**
Can be put in before sex starts. Re-usable (after it is washed).	Must be the right size for you and you need to know how to use it properly. Need to remove and use more spermicide if you have sex again. **Only provides limited protection from cervical cancer and STIs.**
Can make periods regular, lighter and less painful.	Can be seen and can cause skin irritation in some women. **Doesn't protect against STIs.**

Other contraceptive methods

The methods listed below are 99 per cent effective, but need to be administered by a trained health professional. The advantage is they work for longer amounts of time and you don't have to think about contraception each time you have sex.

But NONE of them protects against STIs.

- Contraceptive injection – lasts for eight to 12 weeks.
- Contraceptive implant – lasts for three years.
- Intrauterine system (IUS) – works for five years.
- Intrauterine device (IUD) – works for five to ten years.

Where can I get contraception?

You can get contraception from a doctor, nurse, contraception or 'family planning' clinic, pharmacist or sexual health clinic. Visit the Usborne Quicklinks Website (see page 277) to find out about how to get contraception, along with answers to some FAQs about getting and using it. Most forms of contraception are free on the NHS in the UK.

Emergency contraception

If a woman has unprotected sex (sex without using contraception) or thinks a method of contraception may have failed (a split condom or missed pill, for example), she can take an emergency contraceptive pill. This can be taken up to three days (72 hours) after, but it is more effective the earlier it is taken after having sex.

The emergency contraception pill is sometimes (misleadingly) called the 'morning-after pill' and is available for under 16s from family planning cinics, GPs, contraception clinics, and any of the other places that provide contraception. If you are 16 or over you can also buy it from a pharmacy (without a prescription).

The pill prevents a pregnancy from starting by stopping ovulation (an egg being released from an ovary), stopping the fertilization of an egg, or preventing a fertilized egg from implanting in the uterus. The sooner the pill is taken after unprotected sex, the more likely it is to work.

Did you know?

It's really not a good idea to have unprotected sex because you think you can get the emergency contraceptive pill the next day. It's better for your health to have safer sex using a condom, as this will protect you against pregnancy AND STIs.

How to use condoms

Because condoms are so effective both as a contraceptive method and as the only method that also protects you against STIs, it's very important to learn how to use them correctly. It gets easier with practice, so it's better to try it out for the first time before you start having sex. If you are planning to have sex, practise ahead of time so you know what to do. Some people practise putting male condoms on a banana . . . here's how.

- First check the condom packet is not damaged in any way and that it has the BSI or CE 'kite mark' on it. Make sure you're using the condom before the 'use by' date printed on the packet.
- Open the packet carefully – your fingernails, jewellery or teeth can all accidentally tear the condom inside.

- During sex you need to put the condom on before the penis gets anywhere near the vagina and as soon as the penis is erect (stiff).
- Find the teat or closed end of the condom and gently squeeze it to get rid of air.
- Still holding the closed end, place the rolled-up condom over the tip of the penis.
- With your other hand, roll the condom gently all the way down. (If it won't go down to the base, it may be inside out, so start again with a new one.)
- As soon as the man has come, and while the penis is still hard, he should hold the condom around the base and pull out carefully.
- Wrap the used condom in a tissue or loo paper and throw it in the bin (not down the toilet).
- If you have sex again, use a new condom.

Go to **www.usborne.com/quicklinks** (see page 277) for more information and to see a demonstration.

Top tip

Don't ever use oil-based lubricants such as petroleum jelly, baby oil or moisturiser with a condom as they can damage it. You can buy water-based lubricants from a chemist or supermarket (or use lubricated condoms).

Dumb excuses for not using condoms

If your partner is reluctant to use a condom, you need to ask yourself if you really want to be with someone who cares so little about you that he is willing to put your health and your future at risk.

Turn the page for ideas on how to answer some of the dumb excuses boys may come up with for not using condoms.

Boy: My parents could find out I'm having sex if we use contraception.

Girl: Well, they'll definitely find out you're having sex if I get pregnant – and if they did find out, they might be glad that you weren't taking risks that could affect your whole life.

Boy: Stopping to put on a condom could spoil the mood.

Girl: So do babies! And I can't relax and have sex if I'm worrying about pregnancy and STIs.

Boy: I love you and I'll stick by you if you get pregnant, so don't worry.

Girl: Are you really ready to be a dad? Having a baby is very hard work and puts a huge strain on a relationship. I'm not ready for that.

Boy: Condoms spoil the fun.

Girl: No they don't. Some kinds are really sensitive... and we can make it fun. Anyway, if you won't use one, we won't be having sex at all!

Think tip

Carrying condoms and knowing how to use them doesn't mean you are expecting to have sex, but it does mean that they are there if and when you need them. The only way to avoid STIs and pregnancy is to use a condom every time you have sex.

If you think you might be pregnant. . .

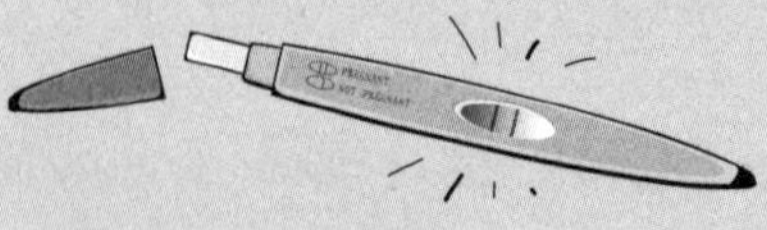

The first signs of pregnancy are usually missing a period, feeling tired, and tenderness in the breasts.

If you have reason to think you might be pregnant, it's very important that you do a pregnancy test, get medical advice and talk to someone as quickly as possible so that you can decide what to do and get the help you need. Go to www.usborne.com/quicklinks (see page 277) to find sources of help and advice.

Sexually transmitted infections

Sexually transmitted infections (STIs) are more common in people aged 16 to 24 than in any other group, so teenagers who have sex without a condom run a high risk of getting an STI or passing one on.

You can't tell that someone has an STI and you can get one the first time you have sex and on any other occasion. You don't need to have lots of sexual partners to get an STI, and anybody who has sex – male, female, straight, gay, lesbian, bisexual – can get one and at any age.

How do I know if I have an STI?

You may show no signs at all, as women are less likely to show symptoms than men. Some common STIs, such as chlamydia, often don't have any symptoms, so you could be infected (and infectious) and not know it, and many people infected with HIV do not have any signs or symptoms initially.

Symptoms of STIs which do show usually appear within 14 days, but they can take up to four weeks to develop. If there are any, the most common signs in men and women are . . .

- Any unusual or smelly discharge of liquid from the vagina or penis.
- Pain or burning when you urinate (pee).
- Itching, rashes, lumps, ulcers, sores or blisters on or around the genitals.
- Pain in the genitals.
- Pain during sex.
- Pain in the lower abdomen, or testicles (for men).
- Bleeding between periods or after sex, or pain in the lower abdomen (for women).

What are STIs?

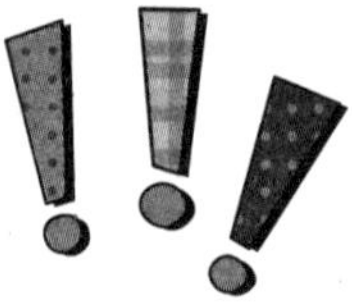

There are more than 25 different sexually transmitted infections. On the facing page are some types and what causes them. The first five in this list are the most common:

Chlamydia	– bacteria
Genital warts (Human papilloma virus or HPV)	– virus
NSU (Non-specific urethritis)	– various causes
Herpes	– virus
Gonorrhoea ('clap')	– bacteria
Trichomoniasis (TV, 'trick')	– parasite
Pubic lice ('crabs')	– louse
Scabies ('itch')	– mite
Hepatitis B	– virus
Syphilis ('pox')	– bacteria
HIV (Human immunodeficiency virus)	– virus

Can STIs be treated?

Most STIs can be treated and it is usually best if treatment is started as soon as possible. Some viruses, such as herpes and HIV (the virus that causes AIDS - acquired immune deficiency syndrome) can't yet be cured, but there are drugs that can reduce the symptoms and prevent or delay the development of complications. If left untreated, many STIs can be painful and can permanently damage health and fertility. And they can be passed on to someone else.

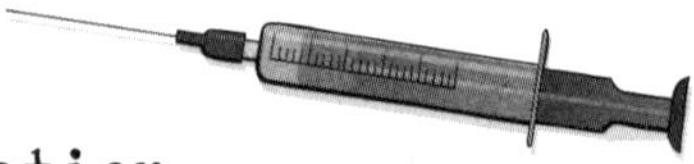

About the HPV vaccination

The HPV vaccination protects against several common and dangerous kinds of HPV and most girls are offered this vaccine when they are about 12 or 13. If you haven't had it, you can still have it up to the age of 18 – ask your doctor or school nurse.

The HPV vaccine doesn't protect against all types of HPV or against any other STIs, so you must still **use a condom every time you have sex**.

When should I get checked?

Even if you don't have any symptoms of an STI, you should get checked:

- if you have had unprotected sex with a new partner recently.
- if you have had sex with another person without using a condom.
- if you know your partner has had sex with another person without using a condom.
- if your partner has an STI.

If you think you could have an STI...

Go to your doctor or a sexual health clinic to get checked. This is free and confidential. There is further information and sources of advice and help at www.usborne.com/quicklinks (see page 277).

Other genital infections

There are some other infections that you can suffer from, even if you haven't had sex. These include cystitis (an infection of the bladder) which causes stinging when you pee, and thrush which causes pain, itching or burning and a white discharge. Both of these are easily treatable, so see your doctor if you have any symptoms.

Thrush can also be spread through sex and cystitis can be triggered by sex, though you can't pass it on to someone else.

> **Remember**
>
> An untreated STI will not just go away and could cause long-term damage to your health. It could even reduce your chances of being able to have a baby in the future. As long as someone has an STI, they can pass it on to someone else.

20. Drink and drugs

As you grow up there will be all kinds of new experiences available to you. Some will be risky, or even dangerous, and there won't always be adults around to 'police' your activities.

Part of your 'mission' as a teenager is to prove you can be trusted enough to make your own decisions and gain some independence. But until your brain has finished developing, you may find it hard to predict the problems that risky activities could cause or assess what could be harmful.

In fact, a part of you may want to try the very things adults tell you can be dangerous, just to show how independent you are, or to rebel against them.

At the same time, every day, your brain is bombarded with messages urging you to try risky things through adverts, films, TV programmes, games, texts, song lyrics, websites, podcasts, tweets, blogs, postings and so on.

Research shows that all this 'advertising' really does work, especially on developing teenage brains. The message your brain gets is: 'Come and try this. It's cool, it's grown-up and fun. Everyone else is doing it . . . so why not you?'

So why not you?

Fortunately, teenage brains, while not very good at assessing risks, are good at absorbing facts. So finding out a bit more about the effects that things such as drink and drugs could have on you, may help you to weigh up the risks, make your own decisions and develop some strategies to stay safe and healthy.

What are drugs?

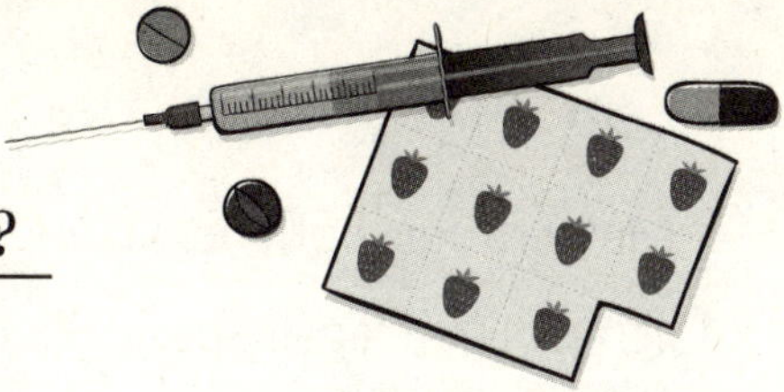

Drugs are chemicals or substances that change the way the body works. When people take them (by swallowing, sniffing, smoking or injecting them) the drugs find their way to the bloodstream and are then carried to different parts of the body, such as the brain. In the brain, drugs alter senses and can make people feel more alert, more relaxed, happier, less anxious, more sleepy or less able to feel pain, for example.

Medical drugs can cure, treat or prevent many diseases, helping people to live happier and healthier lives. But when people talk about 'drugs' in connection with teenagers, they are usually talking about harmful, illegal 'street' drugs, or the misuse of legal prescribed drugs. People take these because they think the drugs will make them feel good, solve their problems, or help them to have a good time.

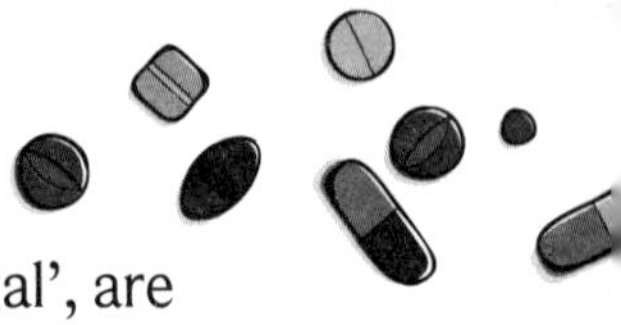

Many drugs, both 'legal' and 'illegal', are addictive. Even legally prescribed medical drugs such as some painkillers and sleeping pills can be addictive, especially if not used in the way they were prescribed. And all drugs have risks and side effects.

Legal drugs include tobacco and alcohol. Illegal drugs include things such as cannabis, speed, ecstasy, cocaine and heroin. There are links to websites which explain more about drugs, all the different names for them, and what they do, at the Usborne Quicklinks Website (see page 277).

Why do people start taking drugs?

- Because they think they will be seen as 'uncool' or won't fit in if they don't.

- Because they hang out with other people who use drugs and don't want to be left out.

- Because they are curious and want to experiment.
- Because a 'friend' tells them drugs are fun.
- Because they think a drug or drink may make them feel more confident and able to face a difficult situation or help them to have more fun.
- Because they are unhappy, stressed or lonely and think that taking drugs or drinking will help them forget or solve their problems.

What are the dangers?

You cannot know for sure what is in an illegal drug as some people who sell drugs mix them with other things, or you may accidentally get a higher dose, which could be harmful or fatal. Turn the page for some of the other dangers linked to drug use.

- Accidents, arguments and fights are more likely to happen after the use of some drugs.

- Using drugs can lead to health problems, addiction, overdoses and serious mental illness such as psychosis or depression.

- Mixing drugs and alcohol is especially dangerous as each one can increase the effects of the other. Mixing ecstasy and alcohol, for example, can lead to dehydration and has been known to cause coma and death.

- Sharing 'equipment' used to take some drugs, such as needles, can spread serious infections such as HIV and hepatitis.

- Drugs are expensive and people who become addicted may find they face financial problems, cannot afford to buy what they need and so end up finding illegal ways to fund their habit.

- Heavy drug users and people dependent on alcohol often drop out of school, become estranged from their friends and family and may end up having nowhere to live.

Did you know?

Between a third and a half of people sleeping rough have alcohol problems and up to 40 per cent of younger homeless people have drug problems.

Tobacco

One of the drugs which people have most problems with is tobacco in cigarettes, even though it is legal to buy (if you are 18 or over). Despite all the health warnings, tobacco is used by over a billion people around the world. This is because every person who started smoking believed that they would be able to stay in control and not develop a habit which is extremely harmful, expensive and very hard to break once someone is addicted.

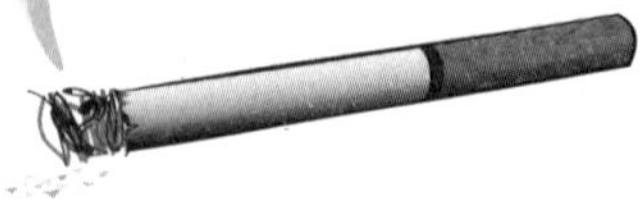

Tobacco in cigarettes kills over five million people worldwide every year. It contains the chemical nicotine which is one of the most addictive substances ever discovered and makes people addicted more quickly than any other drug. In addition to nicotine, cigarettes also contain more than 40 cancer-causing chemicals.

As well as being a smelly and unpleasant habit, smoking is a proven cause of lung, mouth and throat cancers and contributes to many other diseases; it damages the skin, gums, teeth and eyes and it greatly increases the risk of having a stroke or developing heart disease. If a woman smokes while pregnant, she damages her unborn baby's health with every cigarette she smokes.

Remember

The best way of not getting addicted to tobacco, or to any other drug, is not to try it in the first place.

If you hang out with people who use a lot of drugs, you are more likely to develop a habit yourself.

Cannabis

Cannabis (also known as marijuana, weed, dope, hash, grass, blow, pot, draw, skunk, ganja, a spliff, a joint) is the most commonly used illegal drug and many teenagers will come into contact with it at some point. Far from being harmless, it is now known that cannabis is especially damaging to developing teenage brains.

Regular use of cannabis has been linked to physical and psychological addiction, severe depression, thinking and memory problems, sleep problems, anxiety and panic attacks, hallucinations and serious mental illnesses including schizophrenia and bipolar disorder.

Smoking cannabis can also damage the lungs and other parts of the body in the same way as tobacco does.

Did you know?

A recent 20-year study of over 1,000 people found that those who started using cannabis before the age of 18 suffered a significant and **irreversible** reduction in their IQ (Intelligence Quotient) and the more people used it, the greater the reduction.

Another study, of 50,000 people worldwide, concluded that drivers who use cannabis up to three hours before driving are twice as likely to cause a car crash resulting in serious injury or death as those not under the influence of drugs or alcohol.

Ecstasy

Ecstasy (also known as MDMA, E, XTC, pills, tabs, party pills, love drugs, disco biscuits, brownies) is often taken at clubs and parties because it can intensify music and light effects, boost energy and create feelings of belonging, confidence and happiness.

Ecstasy can also cause a faster heart rate, raised body temperature, shaking, dehydration, dizziness, nausea (feeling sick), anxiety and sweating. In the days after taking it, people may feel cranky, lacking in energy, depressed and unable to concentrate.

The long-term effects of ecstasy use are not known, but it is associated with memory problems, anxiety and panic attacks. Accidental overdose or mixing it with other drugs or alcohol can cause convulsions, hallucinations, brain damage and heart failure.

Feeling under pressure to take drugs?

Those are just some of the side effects of a few drugs, but if you're feeling under pressure to take any non-prescribed drug, remember that if you don't use drugs, you're in the majority. Most teenagers DON'T take drugs (maybe because they don't want to become one of the 'stoners' or 'wreck-heads' destroying their brain cells on a daily basis).

It can be helpful to think in advance about how you could respond if someone offered you drugs. If you don't feel confident enough just to say 'no' directly, you could say something like "I've tried it before and don't like it" (even if that's a white lie) or you could just find a reason to leave the situation.

Whatever you say, say it firmly and clearly but don't make a big deal about it. Remember that real friends will respect you more if you are clear about what you do and don't want to do. But if you're finding it hard to be yourself within your group of friends, try to take a step back for a while and think about whether it's time to find a new one . . .

Drinking

Like many other drugs, alcohol is addictive and in the long-term can cause serious physical and mental health problems. Despite this, in many cultures, drinking with friends is seen as a normal and sociable activity for adults. It is associated with relaxation, celebration when things go well or commiseration when things go badly.

So it's not surprising that many teenagers also think that drinking is an appealing and fun activity and are not fully aware of the risks.

There are some very good reasons why, despite it being a legal 'drug', it is not legal to sell alcohol to younger teenagers, and why starting to drink regularly, getting drunk, or 'binge-drinking', especially under the age of 18 when your brain is still developing, is a very bad idea.

One of the reasons is that alcohol affects a teenager's brain differently to the way it affects an adult's. It can actually damage the parts of the brain responsible for thinking, planning, decision-making, impulse control, learning and memory, and the damage can be long-term.

In addition, recent research has found that people who start drinking during their early teens are more likely to become dependent on alcohol, become dependent faster and have more serious problems than those who wait until they are older.

Did you know?

Girls tend to be more easily and more quickly affected by alcohol than boys as their bodies process alcohol differently.

Alcohol is a depressant, so rather than helping you feel better when you are miserable, it can make things seem a lot worse, especially once its initial effects have worn off.

Many experts now say that teenagers shouldn't drink any alcohol at all until the age of 18 and to avoid damaging their brains, they should try not to get drunk until their brains have finished developing in their 20s.

Drinking risks

Being drunk or being where other people are drunk carries all kinds of risks. At the very least, an evening can be spoiled by someone who has drunk too much throwing up, falling over and having to be taken home. But drinking carries much greater risks:

Arguments and break-ups – people often say things they don't mean and fall out with friends and partners after drinking too much.

Car accidents – getting in a car with a driver who has been drinking greatly increases your chances of injury or death.

Violence – the more people drink, the greater the risk of fights breaking out at parties, festivals, on holiday and so on.

Drowning – many drownings happen when people think it would be fun to go swimming after drinking a lot . . .

Unsafe and unwanted sex – girls especially are more vulnerable to sexual experiences they haven't planned, don't want, or haven't fully agreed to when they are drunk. They are also less likely to be protected against pregnancy and STIs.

Alcohol poisoning – in the very worst cases, people can drink so much they have to be hospitalized – or die.

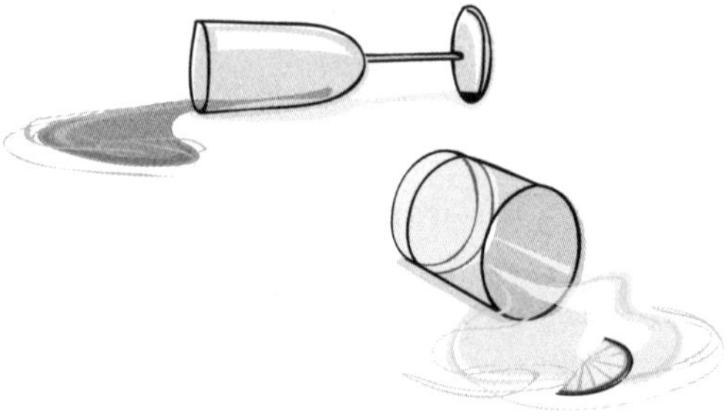

Safer partying

If you know you are going to be around alcohol when you go out, try to remember these guidelines so that you stay safe (and don't wake up feeling as if you want to die . . .). And if you can't remember the guidelines, you've definitely had enough.

- Never drink on an empty stomach and drink plenty of water so you're not thirsty if you have a drink.

- Make sure your phone is charged and you have enough credit to phone a trusted adult who will pick you up if necessary.

- Always go out in a group and stick with your friends. Make sure at least one person agrees not to drink so they can look out for you all.

- If you do drink, stick to one kind of drink and always know how much you are drinking. Drink a soft drink, water or a low-alcohol drink in between any alcoholic ones.

- Don't gulp alcoholic drinks or 'down' them in one go. They are meant to be sipped slowly.

- Avoid strange mixtures, cocktails, alcoholic 'punch', liqueurs and spirits such as vodka.

- Don't accept a drink you didn't ask for from someone you don't know.

- Don't leave drinks unattended at a party or club.

- Never accept a lift from someone who has been drinking (even if they seem sober and say they are fine to drive).

- Don't leave anyone of your group behind, even if they are too drunk to walk, and don't hesitate to call an adult if things are getting out of hand.

- In an emergency, such as someone falling unconscious (so that they don't respond when you try to wake them up), call an ambulance.

What if a friend needs help?

It can be difficult to know how to help a friend having a problem with alcohol or drugs. If you see a friend getting drunk or out of control, you could suggest that they should stop drinking or try getting them to a place where there is no alcohol or drugs.

But don't abandon them or try to talk to them seriously while they are drunk or on drugs. It's best to speak to them the next day and you may then suggest that they get some help (see 'Getting help' on page 236). If you have real concerns and they won't listen, you could speak to a member of their family or one of their teachers.

Do I have a problem?

The most obvious sign that you have a drug or alcohol problem is when you feel you no longer have a choice. You find yourself having to take the drug or drink more and more often to get the same effect and you find it difficult to cope without it. It has become a habit that you are unable to give up.

Quick quiz

To find out if you have a problem, read the questions below and try to answer honestly.

Do you think about drugs or alcohol every day?

Is it hard to say 'no' when they are offered?

Would you drink or take drugs when you are alone?

Does drinking or taking drugs get in the way of the rest of your life?

If you answer 'YES' to these questions, you may be addicted and need to get help.

Getting help

The first step is to talk to an adult you trust such as a parent, your carer, a family member, a family friend, a school counsellor, school nurse or teacher. You could even speak to your GP who can offer advice or may refer you to specialist help.

Go to **www.usborne.com/quicklinks** (see page 277) for other sources of help, advice and information about drink and drugs.

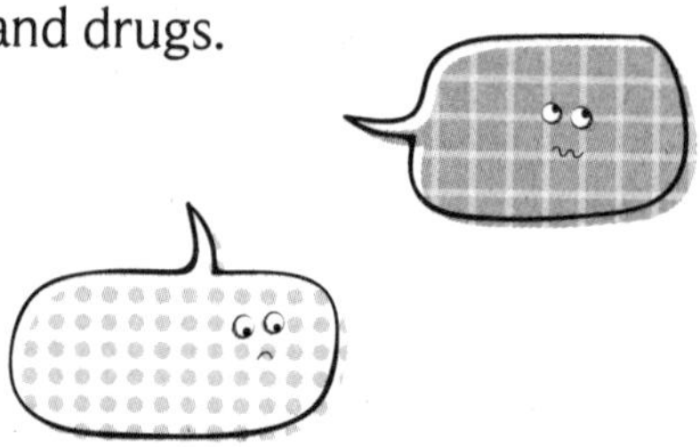

21. Staying safe

Unfortunately the world we live in is not always completely safe, but there are things you can do to help minimize any risks. Here are a few guidelines to help you to stay safe while you are out and about. You probably know most of this already, but, as a teenager, you're more likely to be in situations where there are potential dangers than when you were young. So it's important to remind yourself of the basic rules:

Out and about

- Tell a trusted adult where you are going and what time you are coming back. Phone them before you set off for home from a friend's house.
- Have credit on your phone and make sure it's charged when you go out.

- Know your home phone number and full address.

- Travel in a group whenever possible and stick together.

- Know how you're going to get back and keep enough money for a taxi or bus fare. Only use licensed taxi companies and have their numbers with you.

- Be aware of what is going on around you, especially when crossing roads or on a bike. (Listening to loud music on headphones, chatting or texting on the move makes you less aware of hazards.)

- Avoid potentially dangerous or isolated areas such as quiet pathways or underpasses.

- Never go anywhere with people you do not know, or accept lifts from strangers.

- Don't flaunt possessions such as your phone, tablet, MP3 player or money. Keep them hidden when you are out (not hanging out of a pocket or bag).

- If you need to ask someone you don't know for help, try to approach a family group or an official, such as a police officer.

- Keep phone numbers you can call in an emergency, whether this is a parent, carer, your parent's friend, or a friend's parent.

- Always wear a helmet for cycling, have reflectors on your bike, and working lights if there's any chance that you may cycle after dark.

Internet and phone safety

You may find it hard to imagine that there was any life before the internet and mobile phones as they're so useful for staying in touch, making new friends, finding information and for entertainment.

But, as well as the many benefits, it's important to be aware that there are some dangers associated with using the internet and phones, and to know how to keep yourself safe online.

What are the dangers?

Accessing the internet and using mobile phones can put you at risk of seeing disturbing information or images, being the victim of cyberbullying (online bullying) or being contacted by an adult for sexual purposes (also known as grooming).

There's also a danger of sharing personal information with strangers, sending or receiving sexual messages, videos or images (known as sexting when sent by phone) or getting addicted to social networking or gaming (for example). If you spend too much time online, you just don't get enough exercise and it's also difficult to keep up with all the other things you need to do (such as homework or exam revision, or talking to real people).

To stay safe online:

- Don't share personal information. This includes your full name, photos, addresses, school information, telephone numbers and details of places you like to spend time.

- Make sure you have set your privacy settings to restrict access to personal information.

- Don't give out a friend's details or secrets.

- Think before you publish anything on your profile. Remember it can be seen by anyone (including parents, teachers, future bosses. . .).

- Remember that people online may not be who they say they are. Online 'friends' are still strangers even if you've been talking to them for some time.

- Never meet someone you've met online without an adult going with you. It could be dangerous.

- If you use chat rooms, forums or instant messenger, always use a nickname instead of your real name.

- To stop people accessing your online accounts, keep passwords secret and change them regularly.

- Block people who send you nasty messages, delete messages from people you don't know and don't open unknown links and attachments, as they might be nasty or contain a virus.

- If you see anything that upsets, worries or makes you feel uncomfortable; if you receive any obscene or abusive messages, or if someone you don't know asks to meet you, tell an adult you trust.

- If someone you know is being nasty to someone else online, tell a parent, carer, or adult you trust.

- Don't accept gifts from strangers who have contacted you online.

- Don't use the camera on your phone to intrude on the privacy of others. You could be breaking the law by sending or forwarding such an image.

Take a break

If social networking, gaming or messaging starts to take up too much of your time, you may need a break to stop yourself becoming addicted.

You could try 'deactivating' your accounts for a few days every so often to give yourself a break and see if you can do something else with your time. (You can usually do this in the security area of 'Account Settings'). Deactivation allows you to hide your information as if you had left the site, but you will still be able to turn your account back on with all your friends and information when you want to.

Cyberbullying

If you are being bullied on your phone or the internet, don't ignore it. It can be stopped. The first step is to tell someone you trust who can help you take action. To start with, you could try turning off incoming messages for a couple of days. If you do not respond to messages, the bully may just get bored and stop sending them. If the messages continue:

- You can change your phone number. You'll need to contact your service provider to do this.
- Don't reply to worrying or abusive texts and especially don't send back abusive texts of your own as this could make matters worse.
- Keep records of bullying messages you receive as evidence. Make a note of when they were received and any details you have about the sender.
- If the messages are threatening or malicious and if they persist, get an adult to report them to the site management or the police and hand in the evidence.

Safe from abuse

If someone is hurting you physically, touching you, or making you do something sexual that makes you feel uncomfortable or unhappy, it is NOT your fault and you DON'T have to keep it a secret. You have a right to be safe, at home, at school and when you are out and about.

Tell someone you trust about what is happening. If you are being hurt at home, tell your doctor or someone at school such as your teacher or school counsellor, or call an anonymous helpline. You can't sort this out by yourself, but there are people who can help make your life safer.

Go to **www.usborne.com/quicklinks** (see page 277) for sources of help and advice and to find out more about staying safe.

22. Home and school

Whether you like it or not, during your teenage years you will spend a lot of your time at school, so it's a good idea to develop some skills and strategies for coping with whatever school life throws at you.

As you get older, how you plan and use your time at home also has more and more impact on how you get on at school, especially as you start to prepare for exams and do coursework and homework.

Being prepared

School is always a lot easier to cope with if you are ready for your day. This means knowing in advance what you are going to wear, having homework finished, and leaving yourself enough time to eat a good breakfast and pack your bag with all the things you need. If you are not an early bird and struggle to get up and out of the door on time, you could try some of these strategies.

- Check your timetable and pack your bag each night with the things you'll need for the next day.

- Give any notes, letters and slips from school to your parent or carer as soon as you get them, so they have enough time to reply.

- Lay out the clothes you are going to wear in the evening, so you're not trying to track down a clean shirt, find a missing shoe and stuff toast in your mouth all at the same time.

- Go to bed a little earlier on school nights (see pages 127 to 128 for tips on getting enough sleep).

- If you find it hard to leave on time, set your alarm for a quarter of an hour earlier, so you have more time to get ready in the morning.

- If you need to, work out a bathroom rota with the other members of your family, so you know when your slot is in the morning.

- Make a checklist of things you always need to take (bus pass? lunch card? key? phone? snack?) and check it every day before you leave.

- Make a list of particular things you'll need the next day for school and after-school activities and check them off in the morning (science project? musical instrument? ingredients? PE kit? calculator? dictionary? art book? birthday card for friend?)

Getting the most out of school

As well as your regular lessons, most schools offer 'extra-curricular activities', such as the chance to join clubs and sports teams, go on trips and outings or take part in extra drama, music, dance, science, art or outdoor activities.

All these are good for making new friends, having fun, getting better at things you enjoy, or getting exercise. Don't feel you have to keep up with loads of different activities if you don't enjoy them, but try to stick with ones you do like, if you have the time.

The joy of homework...

The problem some people have with homework is not that they find it too hard, or that it takes too long, but that they forget what they have to do and for when. This may be because they don't write down exactly what needs to be done, or don't make a note of when it has to be handed in.

If you have a planner for school, make good use of it to keep track of what you need to do. If not, use a diary or notebook to make notes of what has to be handed in and when.

You could set up an 'in-tray' system, so you can see what is waiting to be done. This is a tray or shallow box where you put your homework each night until you are ready to do it.

How, when and where?

Although no one exactly looks forward to doing homework, you will get it done more efficiently if you are well organized and have time and space to concentrate on it.

For example, if your homework involves going online and you don't have your own computer, make sure you 'book' some time on the family computer, or can use one in your school resources centre or library, or public library.

If you have space, set up a homework 'office' area at home with a table or desk and a comfortable chair (and as few other distractions as possible). It should have good light, a place for your books, and your homework 'tool kit'. This needs to include:

- Pencils
- Pens
- Rubber
- Sharpener
- Crayons
- Felt-tip pens
- Correction fluid
- Ruler
- Maths equipment (protractor, compass, set square)
- Calculator
- Sticky tape
- Glue stick
- Lined paper
- Plain paper
- Plastic wallets
- Scissors

It helps to get into a routine of doing homework early in the evening, and not leaving it until the last minute at weekends. After you've done it, reward yourself with some fun 'down-time' activities, such as some television or social networking time.

Problems, problems, problems

If you are having a problem at school, or with homework, there is always someone who can help you sort it out. The most important thing (as with any other problems) is to talk to someone.

If, for example, you feel you are being picked on or are disliked by a certain teacher or you are having problems with a particular subject, talk to your class teacher, school counsellor, head of year, your parents or your carer.

One thing many students worry about is bullying at school, whether this is being bullied themselves, knowing what to do if other people are being bullied, or knowing how to stop being a bully if they have become one.

Did you know?

In a recent survey, 46 per cent of children and young people said that they'd been bullied at some point during their time at school.

What counts as bullying?

You don't have to be beaten up or physically hurt to be a victim of bullying. Teasing, spreading rumours about someone, pushing or threatening them are all forms of bullying. Name calling, mocking, taking or damaging belongings, excluding someone from groups and writing or drawing offensive messages about someone are also classed as bullying.

There are lots of reasons why people are bullied. Some people are picked on because of their religion, race or appearance, while others are bullied because of their size, sexual orientation, disability, home circumstances, clothes, or because they're clever – all things that no one should ever be ashamed of.

How does it feel?

If you are being bullied, you may feel as if you're trapped or alone, or that it's hard to make friends or talk to other people of your age.

Bullying can destroy your confidence and sense of security. It can cause sadness, fear, anxiety and poor concentration. Victims of bullying often find that their schoolwork starts to suffer because they're constantly worrying about what might happen at school.

If you're finding it hard to focus on your work and live your life normally, or if you're worried that the bullying is getting violent and you're scared for your safety, you must tell a teacher, your carer or parents. You may find it difficult to talk at first, but it's vital you let them know what's happening so they can help you do something about it.

If you're being bullied, you don't have to put up with it. There are many people that can help you do something about it.

Remember that bullying isn't just something that happens when you're face to face. It can happen over the phone or on the internet too.

See pages 244 to 245 for what to do if you are a victim of 'cyberbullying', or page 176 if you're a victim of homophobic bullying.

> **Think tip**
>
> If you are being bullied, try to remember that it is not your fault and there is nothing wrong with you. It is the bullies who have a problem.

If you see someone being bullied

You may not be affected by bullying yourself, but you may see someone being threatened or teased and want to do something about it.

It's not a good idea to get directly involved with an incident. But don't just ignore it. If you know the person being bullied, encourage them to speak to someone. If you think it will help, mention it to a teacher or parent in confidence, or write an anonymous note. Your school may also run anti-bullying schemes that you can get involved in to help get rid of bullying.

Am I a bully?

Sometimes people are egged on by their friends to bully and they do it because they don't want to be left out. Others feel unhappy themselves for some reason, and take it out on someone else. It takes courage to stop being a bully once you're caught up. But just because you've been involved in bullying, it doesn't mean you have to continue.

Talk to a teacher, parent or older pupil you get on well with. If there's a teacher who's responsible for stopping bullying, he or she should be able to help you. If you don't want to speak to anyone you know, call an anonymous helpline, but do get help for your problem, one way or another.

Visit the Usborne Quicklinks Website for more details (see page 277).

Preparing for exams

Exams are a fact of school life for most people and almost everyone worries about them. The keys to being prepared for exams and avoiding unnecessary exam stress are knowing what you have to learn, planning your revision, and giving yourself enough time to do it. Here are some ideas to help you:

1. Know what you need to do

- If you can, get a copy of the syllabus for each subject. This tells you what you need to know and gives you the topics for revision.

- Find out what form each exam will take, whether written, oral or practical. What sort of questions are there going to be? Essays? Short answers? One word answers?

- Record the dates and times for each of your exams in your planner or diary and make a copy to put on your wall at home.

2. Plan and prepare for revision (about 12 weeks before your first exam)

- Make a week-by-week revision timetable chart to display in your work space. Include the topics you need to cover for each subject.

- Remember to block out times when you can't revise because of lessons or after-school activities. Build in time for relaxation, chores, proper meals and exercise.

- Prepare your workspace. Make sure it's tidy and there's space for all your books, files and stationery. (Check the 'toolkit' on page 253).

3. Start revising

- Start revising early each day, when your mind is fresh. Stick to your timetable and mark off each task as you finish it.

- Build up to working in 45-minute blocks, taking a 15-minute break each hour. Include some longer breaks, and a small reward after a difficult topic.

- Make notes using your class notes and revision guides. Use a separate notebook for each subject.

- Highlight key facts, ideas, definitions, theories etc. Ask your teacher if you don't understand something.

- Transfer some notes, vocabulary etc. onto index cards and use them to refresh your memory.

4. Focus your revision (begin 6 weeks before each exam)

- Practise questions from past exam papers. Look at essay titles, identify key words, list ideas and prepare a plan.

- Vary your methods. Try brief notes, diagrams, pictures, mind maps, flow charts, voice recordings, word games and reading and speaking out loud. Study with a friend and test each other sometimes.

- Cover up what you've written or drawn, write or draw it again and check it against the original.

- Begin to memorize your notes and index cards.

- Ask your teacher again if you don't understand something. It's your last chance to do so.

During your exams

During your exam period you want your brain to work at its very best, so build in relaxation time before bed, avoid late night revision sessions and try to go to bed early so you get enough sleep. If you can, eat regular, healthy meals and healthy snacks and avoid high-caffeine drinks such as coffee, cola and energy drinks.

Check your exam dates, times and places again, confirm your travel arrangements and find out what you can and can't take into the exam room. Then get your equipment ready. You'll need new batteries for your calculator, sharpened pencils and spare pens.

Go through your revision cards during the days before each exam. On exam days leave plenty of time to do everything you need to do and for travel, so you don't feel flustered or too stressed.

Exam tips and techniques

• At the start, read through the whole paper carefully.

• Try not to rush, even if you're nervous. (Try the breathing technique on page 140 if you feel panicky.)

• Check the instructions and underline any key words that show how a question should be answered.

• See how many marks are given to each question and plan how you will use your time. Don't spend too much time on questions that don't give many marks.

• Plan answers carefully, only giving the information you have been asked for.

• Try to answer all the questions that you need to (even if you only have time to make notes for the last one).

• If you can, leave five minutes at the end to check your spelling, grammar and presentation.

Dealing with exam stress

Nearly everyone gets stressed during exams, even if they have prepared well. They worry that they will let themselves, their teachers and their family down or that they won't do as well as their friends or get the grades they need to do the course or job they want to do.

A little stress is useful as it can sharpen your mind and motivate you to do well. But too much stress can stop you working to the best of your abilities, so it's important not to let it get out of control.

As with other types of stress, taking regular breaks and talking to a friend or an adult you trust about how you feel can really help, as can a bit of 'positive thinking'.

Top tip

After an exam, try not to worry about the one you have just taken. Take a break if you can and then focus on revision for your next exam.

Think positive

If you find your mind is full of negative messages, such as 'I can't do this', 'I'm useless' or 'I'm going to fail', try visualizing something more positive. Imagine walking into the exam room feeling calm and confident, turning over the exam paper, reading it carefully and then doing your best to answer the questions.

Then, try to replace your negative thoughts with more positive ones, such as 'I can only do my

> **Did you know?**
>
> A recent survey of 1,300 students found that 96 per cent felt anxious about revision and exams.

best', 'Relax and concentrate' and 'It's going to be OK'. You could even write these on sticky notes and put them around your revision timetable to encourage yourself when you start to feel anxious.

Exercise and relaxation

Learning to relax is vital, both in the run-up to exams and even in the exam room. Try the relaxation routine on page 141 if you find you are getting stressed before exams. Also make sure you build time into your revision timetable for some exercise each day, as this is great for relieving stress.

The breathing technique on page 140 is good for helping to calm you down if you begin to feel nervous or panicky before or even during an exam.

Remember you're not alone. Visit the Usborne Quicklinks Website (see page 277) for links to message boards where you can share your worries with others going through the same experience.

Think tip

Remind yourself that you can only do your best, and your best is all that you can do.

And finally...

Remember that there is life after exams. Things may feel stressful and intense right now, but it won't last forever. And then the rest of your life will still be there, whatever the ups and downs . . . Good luck, and don't forget to enjoy it!

Index

Internet links

The internet is a great source of information about all things to do with growing up, but only if you know where to look and what to believe.

We have selected some useful and fun websites where you can find more information about all the subjects in this book or can access reliable sources of help, support and advice.

For links to these sites go to:

www.usborne.com/quicklinks

and enter the keywords

"growing up for girls"

When using the internet, please follow the internet safety guidelines shown on the Usborne Quicklinks Website. The links at Usborne Quicklinks are regularly reviewed and updated, but Usborne Publishing is not responsible and does not accept liability for the content on any website other than its own. We recommend that all children are supervised while using the internet.

Additional design by Hanri van Wyk
Additional illustration by Candice Whatmore
Additional editorial work by Rachel Wilkie
Additional website research by Jacqui Clark

With thanks to Cassie Cleaver, Eliza Newell, Francesca Malila, Hannah Wood, Helena Dickinson, Katie Davies, Lara Horwood, Lauren Dodman-Edwards, Lia Cox, Lucy Mitchell, Millie Harley, Millie Pardoe, Olivia Brooks, Olivia Treyer Evans and Rachel Wilkie for all their ideas and thoughts about what should be in this book.